DREAM MERCHANT OF THE PERFECT GAME

MASCOT BOOKS
an imprint of Amplify Publishing Group

www.mascotbooks.com

Dream Merchant of the Perfect Game: The Life and Legacy of Frank "Doc" Sykes

The *AFRO American Newspapers* grants permission to republish the image of Frank Sykes in the witness chair during the Scottsboro Boys trials from the article "Dr. Sykes Shakes Ala. Dust and Makes Home in Balto."; Jan. 8, 1938; *Baltimore AFRO American Newspapers*; pg. 24.

The photographs below are published with the expressed written consent of Charles Sykes, a representative of the Sykes family:
Sykes family portrait taken at the Sykes family home in Decatur (circa 1910)
Atlanta Baptist College baseball team (1912)
Howard University basketball team (1916)
Brooklyn Royal Giants baseball team (1916)
Royal Giants—Ridge Grounds—Brooklyn, New York (1916)
Hilldale Baseball Club (1916)
Morehouse College ceremony honoring Doc Sykes as the oldest living graduate (1982)
Family photo on the occasion of Doc's 90th birthday celebration at Howard University (1982)

For more information, please contact:
Mascot Books, an imprint of Amplify Publishing Group
620 Herndon Parkway, Suite 220
Herndon, VA 20170
info@mascotbooks.com

Library of Congress Control Number: 2024920112
CPSIA Code: PRV0824A
ISBN-13: 979-8-89138-238-1

Printed in the United States

For Charles Sykes, the devoted son of an extraordinary man,
and to the entire Sykes family.

DREAM MERCHANT OF THE PERFECT GAME

The Life and Legacy of Frank "Doc" Sykes

BERNARD MCKENNA

MASCOT BOOKS
an imprint of Amplify Publishing Group

PREFACE

"Hey, 'College'; I see you learned how to pitch."
—RUBE FOSTER

On July 24, 1982, Howard University hosted a celebration of Frank Sykes commemorating his ninetieth year and celebrating his remarkable life. The program for that day stated that the "event is a reunion allowing loved ones, kin and extended family to recharge our spirits, break bread, savor precious memories and share the joy of touching again."[1] The attendees included the renowned Afro-American laureates Michael Harper and Sterling Allen Brown. Forty-two years later, Charles Sykes, Frank's son, decided to celebrate his life and legacy once again, and decided upon a biography. Charles's friend, Tim Lavelle, assisted in cowriting this book. As Charles notes, "In conversations with Tim, I mentioned my father several times. Given his interest in the history of baseball, Tim was very interested in the life of Doc Sykes."[2] Tim was familiar with my work on the Black Sox and reached out to me about writing the biography. I thought I knew enough about Doc Sykes, the baseball player, to accept the challenge. I thought I was familiar enough with his testimony in the Scottsboro trial to understand that Frank Sykes played an important role in the case. However, while researching and writing about Charles's father, I grew to be astonished simultaneously at both how little I knew and how his courage and determination shaped history. The more I learned about the man, the more I understood the necessity of a biography.

Frank Sykes's story, which I knew from my research for *The Baltimore Black Sox: A Negro Leagues History*, is crucial to understanding what African American men faced and the sacrifices they made not only to play baseball but to advance the cause of human rights for African Americans. Men like Doc Sykes, whose most productive years came before the formation of the Negro Leagues, contributed to the way African American professional baseball developed independently of the white game. The way Jackie Robinson played ball, which revolutionized the game after his debut in 1947, was born in the first decades of the twentieth century, laying the foundations for the style of Negro League baseball that Jackie learned. Perhaps of more significance, Frank Sykes's testimony during the Scottsboro trials likewise shaped the way the criminal justice system treated African Americans. In short, he played a major role in two revolutions: one in sports and one in law. As such, I begin Frank Sykes's story with highlights of his baseball career and with the story of the Scottsboro case.

Chapter one details two extraordinary games Doc Sykes pitched in September and October 1922. Over the course of five weeks, he threw a no-hitter against the Bacharachs, a team that would become a charter member of the Eastern Colored League. Weeks later, he pitched and won a game against a major-league all-star team. The victories capped an extraordinary year for Sykes. He would win thirty games that season.[3] Against teams that would play in the Eastern Colored League, like the Bacharach Giants, his record was twelve and five, with an earned run average (ERA) of 1.80 and a ratio of walks and hits to innings pitched (WHIP) of 1.01. He allowed only four home runs in "League games," striking out sixty-nine batters while walking only thirty-seven in 159 games.[4] None of these games are part of the official major-league record books—it was a year too soon. Likewise, his victory over a team of major-league all-stars is not part of the official record despite facing Eddie Rommel—who led the white major leagues with twenty-seven wins—and four players who had just played in the white World Series a week before.[5]

Chapter two explores Frank Sykes's role in the Scottsboro trials. The "Scottsboro Boys" were nine young African American men accused of raping two white women on a train. Eight of the accused were tried and sentenced to death within weeks of their arrest. The bias in the case was so obvious that it aroused national—and even international—outrage: Albert Einstein and Thomas Mann were among the signatories to a telegram, addressed to Alabama's governor, expressing concern. They wrote that "in the name of humanity and justice, we beg you to reserve the execution of the eight negroes cast for death."[6] Despite the testimony of one of the women that no rape had occurred, appeals and hearings went on for years, resulting in the acquittal and release of some of the young men, but only after years of incarceration. The other defendants remained imprisoned. Frank Sykes assisted the young men during their years in prison and testified during the trials about African Americans' qualifications to serve on juries. The US Supreme Court ruled, based in part on his testimony, that the Morgan County justice system had systematically and unconstitutionally excluded African Americans from the jury pool. Their verdict in *Norris v. Alabama* revolutionized jury selection procedures across the nation, but particularly in the South. As a result of Frank Sykes's testimony and actions, he was targeted by the Ku Klux Klan, crosses were burned at his home and office, and he and his family faced years of harassment.

Chapter three explores Frank Sykes's family and the community in which he was born and raised: Old Town Decatur, Alabama. Frank Sykes's father, Solomon Sykes, had been born a slave on the plantation of Francis Winfield Sykes. Francis Sykes was also Solomon's father. In the 1880s, Sol Sykes moved to Decatur and opened a saloon and later a funeral home to help support his growing family. They would have seven surviving children. Old Town Decatur was also home to a large working-class and professional African American community. Frank was initially educated in the local schools, but his father sent him to LeMoyne Secondary School in Memphis to finish his secondary education.

Chapter four details Frank Sykes's life as a student at Atlanta Baptist College (Morehouse College) and Howard University. I explore Sykes's college experience in the context of the racial and political tensions of the times: segregation laws, racist attitudes from local and federal government officials, and the traditions of historically black colleges and universities (HBCUs). I offer a context that examines the differing educational philosophies of Booker T. Washington, who tended to favor developing technical skills, and W. E. B. Du Bois, who tended to stress the humanities. I then discuss Atlanta Baptist College during Frank Sykes's time at the school. Within a year after his departure, the college would change its name to Morehouse College. I offer a view of the campus and of student life that a young Frank Sykes would have encountered. I also detail its educational philosophy and the role Benjamin Brawley played in shaping Sykes's decision to matriculate at Howard University in Washington, DC.

When he enrolled at Howard, Sykes focused on his dental studies at the premier HBCU in the nation, one that attempted to respect both Washington's and Du Bois's pedagogical philosophies. Howard, in the first decades of the twentieth century, was also experiencing unprecedented growth. New buildings, including the Carnegie Library, were being built. With Carnegie's philanthropy, money from the federal government came to the school, in part as an act of reparations for slavery. President Taft spoke regularly at important events on campus in the years and months leading up to the 1912 presidential elections. Frank Sykes could not have helped but feel the energy of life at Howard. He also contributed to athletics, playing on both the basketball and baseball teams. He worked as a red cap at Union Station in Washington, DC, where he struck up a friendship with fellow red cap Paul Robeson, the legendary singer, stage and film actor, and political activist.

Chapter five studies the start of Frank Sykes's career (1914–1915) as a pitcher for professional African American baseball teams. It was the equivalent of a summer job with weekend work during the semester. Initially, he proved himself the equal of established stars; but eventually, he would develop into a premier pitcher. He would initially play for four teams: the Brooklyn Royal Giants, the Lincoln Giants, the Lincoln Stars, and the Philadelphia Giants. I offer brief histories of the clubs and explore details of Sykes's performance, highlighting important games.

Chapter six discusses Frank Sykes's final years as a professional ballplayer while enrolled at Howard and his life in the year after his graduation. In 1916, he pitched for the Lincoln Stars during the summer, from June through August. When the semester started at Howard, he pitched weekends for the Brooklyn Royal Giants. His performance was so impressive that, for the 1917 season, Ed Bolden signed Sykes for Hilldale, one of the premier African American clubs in the nation. I offer a brief history of the team and of Bolden's role in developing the franchise, and then share the story of Sykes's time with the club. Sykes would finish his career with Hilldale in the summer of 1918, when he had to report for military service. Unlike some major leaguers whose owners placed them in "essential" industries to avoid military service, Frank Sykes would give up one and a half seasons in the prime of his career to serve his country.

Chapter seven explores Sykes's life in Baltimore from 1920 to 1926. He moved to the city, as evidence suggests, to establish a dental practice and not, at first, to continue his professional baseball career. However, in May 1920, he signed with the Baltimore Black Sox. They, like Hilldale, were one of the premier professional African American teams on the East Coast. Both his dental practice and his reputation as a pitcher grew over the first three years, culminating in his no-hitter against the Bacharachs and his victory over a team of major-league all-stars at the end of the 1922 season. Baltimore became a founding member of the Eastern Colored League in 1923, but Sykes, now thirty-one years old, was past his prime, so his official major-league record reflects the final two seasons of an otherwise extraordinary career as a ballplayer. His dental practice, however, flourished. At the end of the 1924 season, he formally retired from baseball to focus on his patients and on expanding his practice.

Chapter eight examines Frank Sykes's life after his baseball career ended. Sykes returned to Decatur to support his mother and sister after the death of his father. His return to Alabama marks the establishment of his dental practice. I detail the racial climate in the city at the time, the bias in the criminal justice system, and the changing nature of the courts for African Americans, leading up to the Scottsboro trials. During his twelve or so years in the city, he married Alice West, a woman he met in Baltimore, and had three sons. He also thrived professionally, not only as a practicing dentist but in helping with the family's various business ventures. Eventually, he relocated his family to Baltimore, where he could raise his sons in a place they could be relatively free of fear. His dental practice and his family grew. A daughter would arrive in 1946. He continued to practice his profession well into his seventies. He passed away in 1986.

Chapter nine explores Sykes's legacy in baseball, Civil Rights, and through his family. I examine the lasting impact of his career. I detail how his testimony on behalf of the Scottsboro Boys resonates through the history of American jurisprudence, and I look at the lives of his wife and children.

The program commemorating Frank Sykes's ninetieth birthday features excerpts from two poems by Sterling Allen Brown, an African American scholar and poet, who had served as a batboy for Howard University's baseball team when Doc Sykes pitched for them. Like Doc Sykes, Brown's father had been born into slavery, and, like Sykes, Howard University and the city of Baltimore would play important roles in his life. Brown was born on Howard University's campus, where his father was a professor. Sterling Brown would return to Howard as a professor of English. Raised in Howard County, Maryland, he attended Dunbar High School in Baltimore, where Frank Sykes would send his sons. In Brown's "Odyssey of Big Boy," the poem equates the struggles of African Americans to the exile, sufferings, and long-delayed return home of the Greek hero Odysseus. This connection is embodied in "Big Boy," the sometimes gentle but tough-if-you-crossed-him singer who helped initiate Sterling Brown in his first-hand study of the "Black lore" that helped shape his artistic vision. In his odyssey, Big Boy invokes a series of "badmen" or antiheroes to help confront and resist injustice.[7] Brown's tribute to Frank Sykes focuses on the legendary John Henry and Jazzbo. These heroes act in defiance of death, acknowledging its real but also illusory power. Big Boy declares, "When times comes fo' me to go / Lemme be wid John Henry, steel drivin' man / Lemme be wid old Jazzbo." Concluding the poem, these heroes acknowledge that Sykes's life is coming to an end, but with the sounds of a defiant jazz beat and the resonance of a hammer on rock. The momentum of his life is such that, as this invocation of John Henry and Jazzbo suggests, it has shattered the boundaries of death. The corporeal shell may dwindle and vanish, but the spirit and what it created will endure and resonate long after the physical diminishes.

Michael Harper, an African American author who contributed to the event, wrote of the enduring spirit of Doc Sykes in the poem "The Line: How to Step Out of It." Harper describes a boy who "can now stand tall" and of "the klan, on foot or in cars," that now "stand in the womb." Harper writes of Doc having "squired the four freed Scottsboro Boys/out of town in his roadster" and of striking out Josh Gibson. Harper ends his poem by reflecting on Doc Sykes's corporeal shell, telling a reader that it "is ash in the blaze/of a Sunday afternoon," but adding that his spirit is the "Dream merchant of the perfect game." As Harper's poem suggests, Doc Sykes built a spirit that transcends death. Forty-two years after Howard University's celebration of his life, Frank Sykes's legacy endures.

CHAPTER 1

TRIALS AND TRIUMPHS

"He had them gasping for breath."
—***THE AFRO-AMERICAN NEWSPAPERS*, 1921**

For the Baltimore Black Sox, there was no major-league pennant race in 1922; there was no World Series. There should have been. Baltimore should have been buzzing about their Black Sox, who won fifty-three games and lost only nineteen. There should have been talk about Charlie Thomas's brilliant managing, Jud Wilson's batting, and Doc Sykes's pitching that led the team to a championship. Instead, in the American League, the New York Yankees—with Baltimore's own Babe Ruth—would battle the St. Louis Browns for the title. The National League champion, the New York Giants, would defeat the Yankees in the World Series. John McGraw, the hero of the Orioles' National League championship teams in the 1890s, was the Giants' manager. The International League Orioles would win their fourth of seven consecutive titles. It was a good year for baseball in Baltimore, but it should have been a better one. There should have been a pennant race and a World Series for Jud Wilson and Doc Sykes. Charlie Thomas should have been given the chance to manage his team against the Yankees or John McGraw's Giants. There should have been the excitement of a pennant race and a World Series for the Black Sox fans, who crowded Maryland Park, the team's home in Westport. But the Black Sox were a professional baseball club comprised of African American men, so this didn't happen. Even the Chicago American Giants are recognized as a major-league pennant winner for finishing in first place in the Negro National League. For the Black Sox players and fans, 1922 was a year too soon.

The Black Sox did play important games that season. In particular, the late summer and early autumn of 1922 proved eventful for Frank "Doc" Sykes, a practicing dentist and a professional baseball player. On September 10, he started the opening game of a doubleheader for the Baltimore Black Sox against the Bacharach Giants, a rival club in the independent circuit of the top African American professional teams. In 1923, both the Baltimore Black Sox and the Bacharach Giants became charter members of the Eastern Colored League, the counterpart to Rube Foster's Negro National League, which was made up of teams playing in the Midwest, including the Chicago American Giants and the Kansas City Monarchs. For the Black Sox, games against the Bacharachs, Hilldale, the Cuban Stars, the Brooklyn Royal Giants, and the Lincoln Giants had to suffice as a pennant race in the fall of 1922. In what had to stand as the equivalent of a World Series, Sykes took to the mound against a team of white professional all-stars on October 15. It was not yet an official pennant chase or World Series, but the games became a source of pride for the Black Sox and their fans. The pride would extend from the baseball field and into the lives of African Americans, who daily faced pervasive and life-threatening racism and bigotry—a bigotry perpetuated by the white press.

The *Baltimore Sun* targeted Doc Sykes's humanity in May 1923, publishing a cartoon caricature of him. He is sketched in stereotypical "blackface," with large white lips and bulging eyes.[1] The paper would go on to acknowledge and apologize for their history of bias. In a February 2022 editorial, it confessed that they had "treated African Americans as lesser than their white counterparts—restricting their prospects, silencing their voices, ignoring their stories and erasing their humanity."[2] There was no mention of Doc Sykes or of other men and women the paper dehumanized.

To recognize their humanity, we can tell their stories. For Doc Sykes, we can tell the story of his life, of his profession as a dentist, and of his work to build a family and a home both in Alabama and in Maryland. We can tell of his work as a Civil Rights pioneer; he too would face down angry mobs. We can tell the stories associated with his baseball career.

The Bacharach Giants

If baseball betting existed in 1922 as it does today, the betting line would favor offense for the September 10th games between the Black Sox and the Bacharachs. Hitters dream of the kind of conditions that prevailed at Maryland Park that day.[3] Baltimore City's official weather station recorded cloud cover with high temperatures and humidity. Black Sox fans would have known what to expect, as do contemporary Baltimore Orioles fans, who know what happens to baseballs at Camden Yards when summer settles into the areas around the Inner Harbor and Patapsco River. Maryland Park sat about a mile south of Camden Yards with roughly the same field orientation, so conditions would be similar between the two. The probabilities would favor high-scoring games with plenty of hits to keep the crowd excited. Local newspaper coverage helped build that excitement. Unfortunately, the sports pages of *The Afro*, which offered details of those particular games, have not survived. Surprisingly, the *Baltimore Sun* set the stage: "The Original Bacharach Giants, of Atlantic City, will be here today to play the Black Sox, colored champions of Maryland." *The Sun* highlighted what it considered to be each team's star player. For the Bacharachs, the paper declared "Dick Lundy . . . the best colored short stop in the country," and featured "Doc Sykes, star hurler for the locals."[4] *The Sun* covered African Americans in its sports pages with respect and oftentimes admiration, unlike in its news pages. Crowds at Maryland Park included large percentages of white fans in integrated seating. The Black Sox appealed to the entire city, and fans came to that Sunday's doubleheader expecting excitement and "September baseball" (post-season baseball). They would not be disappointed—although they would be surprised.

The probabilities were wrong. Pitching prevailed as it often does in playoff- or late-season games with a title on the line. A deeper analysis of the starting lineups might have predicted that outcome. Doc Sykes pitched the first game for the Black Sox, and Sam Streeter started for the Bacharachs. He would go on to have a sixteen-year career in professional baseball and pitch a 2.40 ERA in 1922.[5] Nate Johnson pitched the second game. His ERA in 1922 was 2.95.[6] The Black Sox sent Talmadge Richardson to the mound in game two. He had a record of nine and three, with an ERA of 2.14 in 1922.[7]

In the second game of the doubleheader, the Bacharachs as a team batted .243 with nine hits in thirty-seven at-bats. The Black Sox batted .258 in that game, with eight hits in thirty-one at bats. They did win the second game five to one, so the hits were timely. The Black Sox also won the first game two to zero, but batted just .148 with four hits in twenty-seven at bats. Future Hall of Famer Jud Wilson, who owns a career .350 batting average, went hitless in both games.[8] The Bacharach Giants were likewise hitless in the first game.

Doc Sykes walked none and struck out two in nine innings. He faced just twenty-seven batters. Based on that information, Bill Gibson, writing for *The Afro* in 1933, called it a "perfect game."[9] Doc Sykes, in conversation with Gibson, called it a "no-hit, no-run game." Sykes was correct. A careful analysis of the box score reveals that Louis Miller, the third baseman, and Blainey Hall, normally the center fielder but playing that first game in right field, each made an error. One runner was eliminated on a double play on a ground ball to the shortstop. The other was likely picked off first, ensuring that Sykes faced only the minimum of twenty-seven batters.

As the quote from that day's *Baltimore Sun* suggests, Black Sox fans expected Sykes to pitch a great game—although a no-hitter and near-perfect game was nonetheless a wonderful surprise. Writing of Sykes in 1921, *The Afro* described him as having "administered the visitors a brand of 'gas' that had them gasping for breath;"[10] the reporter clearly enjoyed deploying a metaphor that referenced Doc Sykes's off-the-field profession. Earlier in 1922, *The Afro* told its readers that Sykes "toyed with the opposition." Sykes was a "spitball pitcher who threw at three speeds—slow, slower, and slowest."[11] The National League banned the spitball in 1919; the American League followed suit in 1920. However, pitchers who had been throwing spitballs were allowed to continue under a "grandfather clause," including Hall of Famers Stan Coveleski, Red Faber, and Burleigh Grimes.[12]

Sykes's performance capped an extraordinary season. His overall record was thirty wins and five losses.[13] Against teams that would play in the Eastern Colored League in 1922, like the Bacharachs, his record was twelve and five, with an ERA of 1.80 and a WHIP of 1.01. He allowed only four home runs in "League games," striking out sixty-nine batters while walking only thirty-seven in 159 innings.[14]

However, one of the great tragedies of Sykes's career was that there were no "League games" in the East in 1922. The Eastern Colored League (ECL) was not founded until 1923. Major League Baseball (MLB) recognized the ECL as a Major League in 2020. Rube Foster's Negro National League (NNL) formed in 1920. MLB recognizes statistics from the 1920, 1921, and 1922 NNL seasons as part of the official major league record. For teams and players in the East, records for those same years are not official in the estimation of major-league baseball. Gary Ashwill and Seamheads.com have scrutinized box scores and news reports to collect records of teams and players in the East for games when they played major-league-caliber opponents, including teams from the NNL and teams that would form the ECL. The statistics are available—the recognition is not.

Doc Sykes suffers perhaps more than any other professional African American player from the period. His peak seasons were in 1920, 1921, and 1922. Against players and teams that would be recognized as "major league," his ERA in 1920 was 1.29, and in 1921, it was 1.93. He pitched for ten years, but after the 1922 season, his abilities declined dramatically, likely due to age and injury. He pitched in thirteen games in 1923 and just nine in 1924.[15] His best years as a pitcher rival any major-league pitcher's three-year peak, but they do not count because of the MLB's decision not to recognize statistics from eastern teams until the formation of the ECL.

His no-hitter against the Bacharachs is also not part of official MLB history, even though eight of the nine Bacharach starters would go on to play in the NNL or the ECL in 1923. The only exception was Preacher Davis, "star third sacker," who did not play after the 1922 season, likely because a line drive hit him in the head, "injuring him severely."[16] Doc Sykes pitched a no-hitter against African American professional baseball players but pitched it a few months too soon for it to be counted as a part of official major-league history. Doc Sykes also proved his skills against white major leaguers in 1922.

The All-Stars

The front-page headline in *The Afro* conveyed bitter irony and rage: "White People Should Stay in Their Places." The story follows remarks by Dr. Robert R. Moton, who was speaking against segregation. Moton was a prominent African American educator who succeeded Booker T. Washington as president of the Tuskegee Institute. Dr. Moton did not support open defiance to segregation, but in his speech in Glasgow, Scotland, in October 1920, he was clear about its evils: "The white people are the ruling, controlling, dominating, directing element. They have the best of everything." Moton added that "Negroes object to segregation because segregation carries with it that the race is inferior and unfit for association with decent people of any other race."[17] The sports pages of that same issue of *The Afro* told the story of both the evils of segregation and the logical fallacy behind it. Doc Sykes had pitched the Baltimore Black Sox to victory against a team of white major leaguers. The African American players proved they were not inferior and demonstrated that, for all the advantages white players had, they did not have the best of everything: the Black Sox were the better team.

Games between the Black Sox and major-league players became an October tradition in Baltimore in the weeks following the World Series. The Black Sox dominated those games. G. M. Gibbs, writing for the *Baltimore Sun* after the 1930 series, stated that he "didn't know whether the All-Stars are convinced that they can't beat the Black Sox but everybody else is."[18] The annual tradition had its origins in a series of games the Black Sox would play against minor-league stars at the end of the season. Doc Sykes had pitched in the last of those games with minor leaguers in October 1921, with *The Afro* remarking that he was in "rare form."[19]

In October 1922, Doc Sykes pitched the first game of what would become a fourteen-year annual tradition of post-season games against major-league white players. Newspaper advertisements heralded the games as the "greatest baseball treat of the season."[20] The fans packed Maryland Park with what was then a capacity crowd of seven to eight thousand.[21] Temperatures were in the low sixties, and the weather, as well as the Major League team, was "unsettled"[22] despite their talent and "advantages." The white team was anchored by Red Sox first baseman George Burns, who batted .306 in 1922 and would win the 1926 American League MVP award. Other players included Ralph "Pep" Young, Ed Lennox, and Frank Parkinson. Hack Wilson may have been the catcher. He did not make his major-league debut with the New York Giants until the following season, but Wilson, who played for the Martinsburg Blue Sox in 1922, became a fixture for the October series between the all-stars and the Black Sox.

The Afro reveled in Sykes's performance, sketching him in cartoon form in sharp contrast to the *Sun's* blackface caricature. In *The Afro*'s depiction, Sykes's pitches zigzag in exaggerated motion toward the plate, baffling the major-league hitters. The sportswriter called him the "Dentist hurler," who "administered a brilliant dose of kalsomine to the All-Star baseball aggregation."[23] A reporter for the *Baltimore American* described Sykes's performance with similar imagery, writing that he "slapped a coat of white-wash on a picked team of players from the American and National Leagues."[24] The imagery in both papers is too consistent not to be deliberate. Just as "blackface" made a farce of African Americans, the whitewash suggests the Black Sox and Doc Sykes embarrassed the white ballplayers.

Written in hindsight, the reporters' enthusiasm is

understandable, but Sykes started the game in less than stellar fashion. He had a rough first inning. Sykes allowed three hits and a walk. The Black Sox committed an error, and only a spectacular play by Richardson, the Black Sox right fielder, saved multiple runs. He caught a liner on the run and threw home to nail a runner at the plate. After the first inning, Sykes settled in, scattering five hits, allowing no walks, and striking out six over the next eight innings. *The Baltimore American* report summed up the clutch pitching of Doc Sykes, writing that the major leaguers "could not fathom the pitching of Sykes in the pinches."[25] As gratifying as his performance was, it's also frustrating to think of what Sykes could have accomplished if he had been allowed to pitch in the major leagues.

The frustration and anger felt when looking at Sykes's performance in the games against major-league players and the Bacharachs reflect the realities of segregation and the culture into which Doc Sykes was born. He fought back on the mound and, with his excellence, demonstrated the logical and moral bankruptcy of segregation. He fought back in other ways as well. When he discovered that the white players were being paid more for the series of games against the Black Sox, Sykes announced that he would not pitch, going to his dental office the morning of Sunday's game. Black Sox management relented and agreed to pay him and his teammates the same as the major leaguers.

He continued to fight racial inequality throughout his life. In the early 1930s, a decade after his playing career ended, he testified in the Scottsboro case, and as Bill Gibson wrote in *The Afro*, "you can bet that took more nerve than it required to set down the

Bacharach Giants in 1922. Yousah!!"[26] The Scottsboro case served as a landmark in the fight for Civil Rights, and Doc Sykes's role in the trial demonstrated his moral leadership and courage.

CHAPTER 2

TO STAND UP AND BE COUNTED

"He wanted to stand up and be counted."[1]
—CHARLES SYKES

Hooded men carrying torches lit up the night sky as they set fire to a wooden cross. The aroma of burning wood and the threat of flames engulfing nearby homes and businesses were both a weapon of war and a symbol of power. For Doc Sykes, that threat was palpable. Crosses were burned both at his home and his office in 1933.[2] The horror experienced by Sykes and his family began when nine African Americans were arrested for rape and assault in Alabama in early spring 1931. They became known as the Scottsboro Boys. Within weeks, all were indicted by a grand jury. Eight were convicted and sentenced to death (Olen Montgomery, age seventeen; Clarence Norris, age nineteen; Haywood Patterson, age eighteen; Ozie Powell, age fifteen; Willie Roberson, age fifteen; Charlie Weems, age nineteen; Eugene Williams, age thirteen; and Andy Wright, age nineteen). Roy Wright, Andy's younger brother, was only twelve. Eleven jurors voted for the death penalty, even for the preteen. One juror voted for his guilt but thought he should be imprisoned for life instead, so Roy Wright remained in custody.

The mainstream white press parroted the official line that the young men were guilty, that they were career criminals, and that it would be better for the community if they were executed. The truth about the case is far more complicated and involves no evidence of a crime, collusion between the mainstream press and government officials at the state and local level, and the loss of the freedom and innocence of nine young men. When the weight of the world was on these teens, the Sykes family, the African American press, and other allies offered them assistance. The US Supreme Court heard appeals. Ultimately, the case would change the jury system in the South. For the African American community, for the young men and their families, and for the Sykes family, the case resulted in lifelong trauma.

The Scottsboro Case: Narratives of Guilt and Innocence

The mainstream white press presented the details of the Scottsboro case as if it were a melodrama, with heroes and victims and the rule of law triumphant. According to the press, state and local officials, including the governor and the National Guard, projected a reasoned calm, order, and strength. *The Chattanooga Daily Times* published exclusive news stories, and the *Associated Press* reports depicted a heroic sheriff, his deputies, and citizen volunteers as bravely facing down a "threatening crowd" of "citizens," while "negroes . . . slept peacefully in the Jackson County Jail." The local authorities had acted decisively when they "arrest[ed] nine for the crime." The governor of Alabama, Benjamin Miller, ordered the National Guard to the jail to support local authorities.[3] The news coverage conveyed trust in local and state authorities, implying that they were capable of unbiased behavior and of ensuring the rule of law. By extension, then, the coverage indicates that any proceedings, including the grand jury and the subsequent trial, also preserved law and order. Indeed, the local and state governments ensured that the "Negroes" could sleep peacefully. The government could be trusted, according to this narrative.

The press presented the young women involved in the incident as poor, innocent girls deserving of sympathy and vicarious outrage on their behalf. They had gone to Chattanooga seeking work. Not having enough money for the return trip home, they boarded a freight train with a relative, his friend, and five other young white men. The girls changed into overalls before boarding the train. They took precautions; they were not dressed provocatively; and they had a trusted escort. They were also raped: "outraged innocence at the hands of negro men," the newspapers reported. Even though they were "sobbing" as they lay in a hospital, they told a "coherent story" of being raped at "knife-point." The newspapers published the women's names and as much of the details of the incident as they could, calling them "girls from Huntsville."[4] They personalized the story for their readership. They could be anyone's daughters; they were innocent victims.

The white newspapers also had heroes and villains for their narrative. Of the seven "white boys" who were traveling with the girls, five were allegedly forced from the train at gunpoint. The "negro men" knocked the other two unconscious before commencing the assault. After one boy recovered consciousness, he fought back but was overpowered and made to watch the girls being raped.[5] The villains were the accused. The newspapers declared their guilt before the trials: "Nine blacks outrage two white girls," read the headline. The subheading told readers that "the blacks accomplish[ed] their fiendish purpose."[6] The Chattanooga papers described them as "notorious" and as a "gang." The "colored people of South Chattanooga fear[ed]" them, and they "had harassed city officers for months."[7] For the mainstream press, speculation reinforced their narrative.

The African American press presented a different perspective. The *Associated Negro Press* (ANP) offered the story of a passive government responding with a minimum amount of action rather than the trusted authority intent on maintaining order and upholding the rule of law, as portrayed by the white press. In fact, the news stories credit a "drop in the temperature" as having "saved nine men from being lynched." The white press also credited the weather but put the credit primarily on the authorities, with the temperatures as a secondary factor. The ANP version of the news story also emphasized that the confessions the African American men offered were the police version, writing that "according to the police, six . . . immediately confessed." The change in emphasis suggests doubt that the official version is accurate or, if accurate, reveals that it was the police that focused on immediate confessions obtained without legal representation. The story also presents the governor's response to the situation as passive rather than authoritative: "Local officers had requested help from the governor and a detachment of troops was sent."[8] Details also emerged regarding the governor's action. After that first day, reports in the African American press revealed that the prisoners were left "without protection."[9] Ultimately, rather than a sense of calm and order, "a mob atmosphere pervades the place."[10] The differing representations of governmental response and credit at the local and state level represent the different experiences with authority in the African American communities and the white communities, particularly in the South. For African Americans, the issues involved distrust and suspicion. The white press, in their narratives, dismissed those concerns.

The African American press also exercised more restraint in covering the details of the case. Stories only mention the accusers after the initial court proceedings. Before the verdicts, the ANP delicately handled the accusations, writing only that, "According to physicians who examined the girls they were not badly hurt."[11] The implication is clear: The girls were not raped. When the African American press did finally disclose the girls' names, it did so by citing their source: "International Labor Defense investigators secured the names of the two girls who brought the charges and gave them as Victoria Price and Ruby Bates. It is said by these investigators that these girls are of questionable repute."[12] The stories question the girls' testimony, presenting facts and sources for the information.

The ANP also did not mention the white boys until after the trial's conclusion. Rather than representing them as defending the girls, ANP accounts describe them as instigating a confrontation, but the accused had "got the best of their opponents." Humiliated, the white boys leapt from the train, abandoning the girls, and concocted the story, which was sanctioned and spread in the white press. Once again, African American lives were sacrificed to spare white men's humiliation. The ANP stories also did not entertain the rumors and speculation regarding the Scottsboro Boys' supposed criminal past.[13]

Not surprisingly, the white-press narrative prevailed, and justice was swift. By March 30, a grand jury indicted the young African American men. Between April 6 and 9, the court held four separate trials, convicting all but one of the accused. The sentence for the Scottsboro Boys was death, to be carried out in July. The narrative was complete: The two young girls could rest secure knowing that the government would take care of those responsible for their loss of innocence. According to the narrative, the government upheld the rule of law and due process, protecting the rights of the accused and those who suffered humiliation and assault. Heywood Patterson, one of the condemned boys, was just seventeen. He wrote to his parents, begging for help: "My dearest mother and father, this is to let you know of my present life. I am worried to think that your poor son is going to die for nothing. Do all you can to save me from being put to death for nothing. Mother, do all you can to save your son." There was little their parents could do, however. "Mr. Patterson, Heywood's father, work[ed] in a steel mill . . . three days a week, earning $7 a week for a family of 8."[14]

Although the mainstream narrative would not stand up to scrutiny, the injustice continued. The African American press and men like Frank "Doc" Sykes would speak against it and against the system it attempted to sustain. Without Sykes, the ANP would not have been able to tell the story of the Scottsboro Boys. He "rendered valuable aid to William N. Jones and P. Bernard Young, the only colored newspaper correspondents in Decatur when the trial started." Sykes moved "the reporters from house to house when the situation for them became threatening." The Ku Klux Klan confronted Sykes and the reporters directly when they attempted to contact a reporter for the white press.[15]

Appeals, Threats, and Intimidation

Because the African American press was able to tell the story of the Scottsboro Boys, outrage ensued. In June 1931, the boys received stays of execution, pending an appeal to the Alabama Supreme Court, which, in early 1932, upheld the convictions and sentences. However, the United States Supreme Court agreed to hear the case and issued a ruling (*Powell v. Alabama*) that the case should be remanded to a lower court because the defendants were denied counsel. During the retrial, one of the young women, Ruby Bates, testified that no rape had taken place. Despite her testimony, the jury voted to convict the young men. However, during the retrial, Samuel Leibowitz, a lawyer from New York who had agreed to represent the defendants, questioned why there were no African Americans on the jury. He called Frank "Doc" Sykes to testify. Sykes and his family had provided material support for the Scottsboro Boys accused from the start of their ordeal. As Sykes's role in the case became more prominent, so too did the wrath of the white supremacists. His testimony would "upset the Alabama jury system and have repercussions throughout the South."[16] He would pay a high price for his work.

Sykes's court appearance, as shown in the photo that accompanied the story in the African American press, featured a display of dignity set against the theatrics of abuse. His clothing could be that of an English gentleman: a double-breasted suit, a dark tie, a white shirt, turned-up cuffs, and derby boots. He wore wire spectacles, modeled a neatly trimmed chevron mustache, and sported close-cut hair. He crossed his legs at the knee, and his body relaxed into his chair. The only suggestion of tension lay in his hands, which held a list of names on paper. He could be settling in for an evening's conversation over after-dinner drinks at a fine restaurant in London or New York, but Sykes was in an Alabama courtroom, testifying in an effort to save the lives of eight young men.

Frank "Doc" Sykes testifies during the Scottsboro case (1933).

A rail stands behind him with a single bar rising just about twelve inches above the floor. Behind the bar, and set against Dr. Sykes's dignified presence, white men spit tobacco onto the floor near a spittoon. Reports suggest they purposely missed their mark so their excretions would land near Dr. Sykes. Behind him sits the spitting man, and, near him, other men howl in laughter and gesticulate. Their feet rest on the bar with their legs spread and their upper bodies leaning forward toward their ankles. They too wear suits, but without Dr. Sykes's dignity. Their trousers rise above their socks, exposing their ankles. In what could be a scene from *Théâtre de I'absurde*, they appear as animals while Dr. Sykes retains his humanity. Unknowingly, the howling men reverse the cruel stereotype of African Americans. The white men's simian behavior showcases Dr. Sykes's civilized demeanor.[17]

Frank Sykes held in his hands a list of 120 names. The jury pool for the Scottsboro trial excluded African Americans on the pretense that they were not intellectually capable of understanding the process. The defense presented Dr. Sykes and others to demonstrate that African Americans had intellectual capacity equal to that of white men. In addition to his testimony proving his intellectual capabilities, he offered the court a list of African American men who could also be included in the jury pool.[18]

Demonstrating a dry wit that belied the horror of his testimony's aftermath, Frank Sykes told Norfolk's *New Journal and Guide* that the "air is still a little hot" in Decatur.[19] At first hearing, he could be discussing the heat of late spring in Alabama or even using a metaphor to describe the heated atmosphere following his testimony. Indeed he was—but he was also using his sardonic humor to discuss what happened to him and his family after he had spoken to the court. "Whites" bragged that they would "take care of the witnesses." The Ku Klux Klan burned crosses in front of his home and offices.[20] It would not be the last threat against Frank Sykes and his family.

However, two years after he testified, the United States Supreme Court ordered another retrial in the Scottsboro case based on the exclusion of African Americans from the jury. The case *Norris v. Alabama* ruled that the defendants' rights to equal protection under the Fourteenth Amendment had been violated. The ruling prompted changes in the jury selection process in Alabama and throughout the South.[21] Sykes, his family, and supporters of the Scottsboro Boys had won a battle in their war for the rights of the young men.

They would win another battle in the retrial. In July 1937, the cases against four defendants (Olen Montgomery, Willie Roberson, Eugene Williams, and Roy Wright) were dropped. The judge immediately advised the defense to get the four young men out of Alabama as quickly as possible before "word spreads" of their freedom.[22] Dr. Sykes and his family arranged for two cars to drive to Chattanooga, where the young men would take a train to New York. Frank Sykes himself drove one of the cars and then returned to Decatur. He had been warned "by the leaders of a blood-thirsty mob bent on vengeance on the liberated boys that 'If you do not stop fooling with that Jew from New York [the defense attorney], they will find your body in the river.'" The *Chicago Defender* reported that he and his family were the "unknown hero[es] of the Scottsboro case." They had provided for them "the entire six years they were incarcerated."[23] The African American press picked up the story and spread the news nationwide. The *Baltimore Afro-American* spoke with pride of Doc Sykes's connections with the city, mentioning his career with the Black Sox.[24]

The white press presented a different version. During the trial, the *Evening Sun* mentioned Frank Sykes once, referring to him as a "Negro dentist" who "read to the court a long list of Negroes residing in the County whom [he] believed qualified for jury duty." The story characterizes Sykes's testimony as an "attack" on "Alabama juries."[25] Thirty-six years later, in a review of a book about Scottsboro, Benjamin Quarles, a history professor at Morgan State University, wrote for the *Baltimore Sun* that "Sykes courageously presented to the hostile trial court a roster of the names of local Negroes who, in his firmly stated opinion, met the qualifications for jury service."[26] The *Baltimore Sun*'s belated recognition of Sykes was most certainly welcome, especially as it was written during the height of the violence surrounding the Civil Rights Movement in the late 1960s.

The belated recognition, however, emphasized the cultural divide between the African American community and the white community. It also emphasized Frank Sykes's courage.

Epilogue

Five young men, however, remained imprisoned. Charlie Weems was retried and sentenced to serve seventy-five years. He was paroled in November 1938. Andy Wright was sentenced to serve ninety-nine years, but he was paroled in 1944. Ozzie Powell's rape conviction was eventually set aside. However, he was sentenced to serve twenty years for assaulting a sheriff's deputy. He was paroled in 1946. Heywood Patterson was sentenced to seventy-five years in prison. He successfully escaped in 1948 and subsequently killed a man in a bar fight. Convicted of manslaughter in 1951, he died in prison a year later. Clarence Norris was sentenced to death, only to have the sentence commuted to life in prison. He was paroled in 1944. In 1976, George Wallace, then governor of Alabama, pardoned him. Clarence Norris lived until 1989, the last of the Scottsboro Boys.

Doc Sykes's role in the Scottsboro case is acknowledged, although not fully appreciated. Dan Carter, in *Scottsboro: A Tragedy of the American South*, described him as "a handsome man" who was "polite but ostentatiously self-confident" during his testimony.[27] Peggy Allen Towns described him as "self-confident" and "calm" in the face of ridicule.[28] Sheryll Cashin notes that Sykes's "immodest self-confidence . . . spurred the Ku Klux Klan to burn a cross on his front lawn as a warning for violating a Southern code that depended for its efficacy on Negro submissiveness."[29]

What motivated Frank Sykes? In 1990, his son Charles told *Baltimore Sun* reporter Bill Glauber that his "father felt a sense of responsibility and duty, a sense of community. . . . He wanted to stand up and be counted."[30]

CHAPTER 3

"THE FLOW AND UNITY OF THE COMMUNITY"

FRANK SYKES'S FAMILY AND THE AFRICAN AMERICAN COMMUNITY OF OLD TOWN DECATUR, ALABAMA

It's a Saturday morning. It could be anywhere in the United States. Parents get their children ready for that day's baseball game. They make sure the kids have their uniforms, bats, and gloves. They pack water and a snack. There's excitement and more than a little stress involved in making sure everyone gets out of the house on time. In "Old Town" Decatur, Alabama, families come together at the William "Butch" Matthews Field, located on Grove Street, just as it bends to the northwest. Trains run along the tracks behind home plate, creating a distraction for the young baseball players. The field sits a few blocks away from both the Tennessee River and Old Town, the heart of Decatur's historic African American community.

From the field, it's a ten-minute walk to the place Frank "Doc" Sykes grew up and where he opened his dental office in 1927. Urban renewal projects in the 1970s razed many of the old homes and buildings, but the young ballplayers and their families can at least visit the places where those structures once were. They can get a sense of the street where Doc Sykes likely played catch with his brothers, sisters, father, and mother. It's probable that he learned to pitch within spitting distance of Matthews Field. The man who would no-hit the Bacharach Giants and befuddle major league all-stars undoubtedly had his first strike out here.

The Scottsboro Boys tour starts at the Morgan County Courthouse. Frank Sykes's adult home, at 812 Well Street NE, is the second stop. Just as his former home shapes the way visitors interact with Decatur's historic landscape, Old Town and his family shaped the ballplayer and the man that Doc Sykes would become.

Old Town

Old Town Decatur, Alabama, where Frank Sykes was born and raised, has a rich African American history. In addition to the Scottsboro Boys tour, the Freedom Pioneers offer the Tommy Lee Hines tour, with stops that showcase the contributions of African Americans to Decatur. Tommy Lee Hines was a "young, black, intellectually disabled man" accused of raping three white women in 1978.[1] Even though "the preponderance of evidence established it was impossible for the accused to commit these crimes," he was convicted and sentenced to thirty years in prison. His case has echoes of the Scottsboro Boys, and the tour chronicles an African American community's resistance to racism and bigotry in Decatur. The tour also commemorates African American-owned businesses and other achievements of Old Town's Black community.

Old Town was one of many African American communities in the South that began to prosper in the late nineteenth and early twentieth centuries. In Baltimore, African American businesses flourished along Druid Hill Avenue, where Doc Sykes would make his home during his Black Sox career. At first glance, such prosperity seems impossible in a heavily segregated South, with laws and bigotry limiting economic opportunities for African Americans. However, it was just these circumstances that allowed Black-owned businesses to take root:

> Even though blacks in the South were wretchedly poor individually, collectively they formed a sizable market. African American entrepreneurs opened corner grocery stores, corner saloons, billiard halls, beauty parlors, barbershops, and funeral homes. They seldom faced competition from established white-owned companies, which refused to operate in black neighborhoods. From these small beginnings, black business districts emanated, forming the backbone of new black communities.[2]

The African American community in Old Town was accustomed to resistance. Decatur was occupied by Union troops for much of the Civil War, and two regiments of Black soldiers were raised in the city.

Many of the places that were significant to the history of African Americans in Decatur fell victim to decay and neglect, and, ultimately, "most of the structures in Old Town were demolished during the city's urban renewal project during the 1970s."[3] Frances Tate, an artist who chronicles African American buildings in Old

Town, derisively called the movement "urban removal." The actual buildings no longer exist, but the history of Old Town as a thriving community during Reconstruction and Jim Crow is far more difficult to erase. Indeed, historic evidence tells us that it became "the centerpiece of Decatur's Black community during the Jim Crow era."[4]

Old Town was founded in the 1820s, and along with the white settler community came slaves, who built the oldest standing buildings. During the Civil War, Union troops occupied Old Town, and many of those slaves and their descendants joined the Union army.[5] After the Civil War, freed Blacks settled in the area formerly occupied by the Northern regiments. Just as desegregation caused "white flight" in the 1950s and 1960s as African American families moved into one area, "after the reconstruction of Decatur, many of the white families moved out of Old Town and moved to old Decatur." Nonetheless, "after the Civil War, Old Town began to emerge politically and economically. New employment opportunities attracted former slaves and their families to the area."[6] In relative terms, Old Town was prosperous and, in certain terms, offered a sense of community.

In the years after the Civil War, schools and eventually African American doctors, lawyers, and dentists came. As Peggy Allen Towns observes, "There were educational opportunities, too, albeit rigidly segregated ones, and by the turn of the century, Old Town boasted a sizeable population of Black professionals. A former slave and Confederate army veteran helped to found the first public school in Old Town: Matthew Hewlett Banks . . . and other Old Town men petitioned the Decatur City Council to provide a school for African American children."[7] A few years later, residents established the first private school at St. Stephen's Primitive Baptist Church. The school would later move to St. Paul's Methodist Episcopal Church. The schools would help to form a literate African American community, which would, in turn, foster other local enterprises. In the early twentieth century, Eva Young Sterrs founded *The Guardian* (1910–1917). It was, unselfconsciously, "a black newspaper, published monthly that featured social, religious and cultural news."[8] Although short-lived, the paper nonetheless demonstrated that in the post-reconstruction Jim Crow era, African American communities were literate and had a clear sense of values, customs, and beliefs.

Old Town also served as the home for a hospital and nursing school. By the turn of the nineteenth and twentieth centuries, the Cottage Home Infirmary and Nursing Training School established a reputation as an elite institution—not only for African Americans but for the medical profession in the South and, indeed, nationwide. Founded by Dr. W. E. Sterrs, whose wife started *The Guardian*, the hospital was "an established hospital that offered some of the best medical treatment in the nation." Dr. Sterrs, in the estimation of Peggy Towns, "likely moved to Decatur because he saw 'possibilities and opportunities' in a thriving black community."[9] Sterrs "treated people 'regardless of race or whether they had the means to pay,' . . . And, at one point, officials with the all-white Ladies Benevolent Society of Decatur requested that some of its nurses receive training at Dr. Sterrs' nurse training school."[10] Cultivated within the segregated community of Old Town, the hospital's excellence served as a tool for integration in the South.

The hospital also provided emergency services. Dr. Sterrs

offers a description of one instance:

> A young man, "age 22, in a fight was stabbed in right side of neck. [The] patient ran across the street to my office holding as best he could the spurting wound. Seeing the blood spurting in a large current and thinking that only a few more would end his life, I seized the wound with my hand and let him down on the floor at once. Finding I could not control the hemorrhage neither could I catch the bleeding vessels through the opening in the neck which was about two inches long I sent for assistance. To remove the hand I held on the bleeding point and release my hold would be followed at once by the same gushes."

Dr. Sterrs and his nurses were able to stop the bleeding and stabilize the young man.[11]

Writing in *The Journal of the American Medical Association* (1919), John Kenney saw Cottage Home as "a small training school, but a very excellent one." The Cottage Home's nursing school graduates, Kenney notes, are working "in different parts of the state of Alabama, and are doing 'admirably' well."[12] The *Journal* also offers a detailed history of the training school, noting that "the infirmary opened in a three-room cottage in 1900, and within a decade, was a two-story building with 18 rooms. . . . The first nurses graduated from the training school in 1910 and, according to the medical association, 'quite a variety of cases, both medical and surgical, have been treated in this institution with credit to its management and nurses.'"[13]

The History of Old Town

To help express the complex history of Old Town, contemporary artist Frances Tate uses water from the Tennessee River to create her paintings because the river represents the "flow and unity of the community."[14] That community confronted systemic racism and bigotry, fighting significant battles throughout its history, notably the cases of the Scottsboro Boys and Tommy Lee Hines. The African American community also created business and religious congregations. They raised strong families with a deep-seated sense of pride and dignity. When Frank Sykes testified before the court, advocating for the Scottsboro Boys, he conducted himself with that same dignity, nurtured by his family and by the Old Town community. Frances Tate's watercolors preserve and reflect that pride. Old Town's story is also the story of African American entrepreneurs in the South at the turn of the nineteenth and twentieth centuries, as John N. Ingham notes:

> African American businessmen and women . . . overcame staggering odds. Having little in the way of capital, education, or business training, and facing deep-rooted, often legislated racism, ex-slaves and children of slaves created a new group of enterprises. Unlike earlier black businesses that relied on patronage from the white community, these new endeavors served African Americans, often out of necessity. The largest and strongest districts generally evolved in cities that contained large, homogeneous African American neighborhoods. These neighborhoods concentrated the population, so that, despite the meager earnings of most blacks, it was

> possible to establish successful groceries, barbershops, beauty salons, saloons, pool halls, and other small businesses. It is a great irony that the evil of Jim Crow, under which black Americans were subject to segregation, humiliation, and persecution, encouraged black capitalism to flourish.[15]

Ingham's research does not specifically mention the Sykes family or Decatur, but the references to saloons and funeral homes and to the emerging professional classes of lawyers, physicians, and dentists tell the story of that extraordinary family. As Peggy Towns observes, "We stand on the shoulders of our ancestors who actually built this town . . . and I think that needs to be recognized."[16] Frank Sykes and his family are part of the community of Old Town, deserving recognition. In turn, that community formed him and influenced the man he would become.

The Sykes Family

Frank Sykes was born on April 10, 1892, and grew up in a large family in a close-knit neighborhood in Old Town. He was one of seven children. Newman and Leo were his older brothers, and Carl and Melvin were his younger brothers. His two younger sisters were Estelle and Ernestine.[17] His father, Solomon Sykes, ran a saloon a few blocks from his home. His mother, Ada, ran the very large household. Ada's sister, Mary Garth, also lived with them; she was a teacher.

Frank's neighbors in the African American enclave of Decatur were a mix of working- and upper-middle-class families. Census data gives a picture of the types of work the neighbors did. Thomas Bynum, Will Mitchel, and Preston Rogers worked as laborers in the railroad freight office. Robert Bridgeforth was a liveryman, and Edward Jones was a waiter at the hotel. Willie Evans, like Frank's Aunt Mary, was a teacher. H. L. Murphy owned the local grocery store, and W. J. Smith was the minister of the Methodist-Episcopal Church. Frank's uncle and next-door neighbor, J. J., was a coal merchant.[18]

Without exception, all the adults in his local community could read, and all but one could write. In this sense, Old Town was an aspirant model. As James Anderson points out: "Blacks emerged from slavery with a strong belief in the desirability of learning to read and write."[19] For those communities, "Being educated and literate had an important cultural significance to African Americans, and they pursued these goals in opposition to the economic and ideological interest of the Planter-dominated South."[20]

The reality for most African Americans in the late nineteenth century was starkly different from that of the residents of Old Town. Nationwide, Black literacy was only 52 percent in 1900.[21] Also, without exception, all of the children between the ages of six and sixteen in Frank Sykes's neighborhood went to school. In Alabama as a whole, in 1900, only 46 percent of boys and 55 percent of girls went to school. Yet none of the children sixteen or younger in Sykes's neighborhood worked. In African American Alabama communities at that time, 57 percent of boys and 35 percent of girls worked full or part time.[22] Old Town Decatur offered Frank and his brothers and sisters an environment that valued them, fostering their intellectual and social development.[23]

Frank's mother and father were married in Decatur on January 15, 1880.[24] The census describes his mother as "Black" and his father as "Mulatto." Ada was born in 1862, which means she was born into slavery, the property of the Garth family. Solomon Sykes was also an enslaved person. He was born in 1855 on the Sykes family plantation. Dr. Francis Winfield Sykes ran the plantation and owned Solomon and fifty-seven other African Americans.[25] Dr. Sykes was also Solomon's biological father. Solomon's mother was Laura Garth, also an enslaved person, on F. W. Sykes's plantation. She was described as "beautiful" and was a "wedding present" for Dr. Francis Sykes. Laura would go on to bear six of Sykes's children.[26]

Francis Winfield Sykes was born in Decatur on April 19, 1819. He trained as a physician and inherited the family's plantation after his father's death in 1849. He married Susan Elizabeth Garth, whose family owned Ada Garth Sykes, on January 27, 1844. Together, he and Susan had four children. F. W. also sired at least seven other children with women he held in slavery.[27] In addition to running his family's plantation and his work as a physician, he was also a politician, serving in the Alabama state legislature. Politically, he was a Southern Unionist and a member of the anti-immigration American Party, the self-proclaimed "Know Nothings."[28] At political rallies, he was able to stir up a crowd into what the newspapers called "the greatest outbursts of . . . enthusiasm." He spoke with "great force" and with a "sledge hammer and knock down, drag out" style.[29] When he died in 1883, the *Alabama Courier* described his passing as "a real loss to his family, his friends, his county and his State."[30]

After Emancipation, Solomon worked on his father's land, but within a year of his father's death, Solomon and Ada moved to Decatur. In Decatur, Solomon and Ada would open a saloon and establish their family. The 1880 census tells us that they lived with Solomon's brother, Melvin, and that all three worked as farmers. Solomon was the head of the household. His father had given each of his children—along with Laura Garth—farmlands; it's likely that Solomon sold his interests in the farm for the money to move to Decatur and open a saloon.[31]

Sykes family portrait taken at the Sykes family home in Decatur (circa 1910).

A contemporary reader may have some preconceived and even misconceived notions of what a saloon means for the community. There is and was a bias against bars and saloons, born of the Temperance Movement, with the misconception that they served as centers for excessive drinking and violence, clearly stoked by the media. Solomon Sykes did have to battle those headwinds. In 1890, *The New Decatur Advertiser* reported that "Lawrence County's scallawags [sic] and scoundrels come to Decatur to do their devilment." That the paper meant African Americans is clear. The story details only crimes by "colored" and "negro" men, offering specific details on one particular incident: "Bob Levert, a well known negro of Decatur, got into an altercation Christmas morning in a saloon on Bank Street, run by Sol Sykes, also colored. Levert shot twice at Sam Barker, colored, wounding him in the left shoulder and arm. One bullet also hit a negro bystander in the calf of one leg."[32]

Another news story from the *Birmingham Post Herald* linked Solomon's saloon to "suspicious circumstances" in the deaths of two men. The paper concedes that it was reported that the men died of "heart disease" and "overindulgence." The man drowned in the river after leaving the saloon in a drunken state. However, the news story points out that one of the men "was seen near the river in the company with another negro only a few minutes before being picked up dead." The two deaths in close proximity, the newspaper tells its readers, gives "the whole affair a mysterious coloring." The *Post Herald*'s choices to point out the race of the man seen near the river and its use of the word "coloring" were intended to use racial stereotypes and a bias against alcohol to disparage Sol Sykes and his business.[33] A year earlier, a patron of the saloon stabbed a policeman, and the officer shot and killed his assailant.[34]

Nonetheless, Skyes's saloon played an important role in the community. The saloon functioned as a "social center." An article from the 1897 issue of *the American Journal of Sociology* argues that the saloon "supplies legitimate needs and stands alone in supplying them. It transforms the individual into a socius where there is no other transforming power. It unites the many ones into a common whole which we call society, and it stands for this union amid conditions which would otherwise render it impossible."[35] More recent scholarship, discussing the role of the saloon in late-nineteenth-century America, points out that it was often "a neighborhood center" and a "transmitter of working-class and immigrant cultures."[36] Sol Sykes's place of business played an important role in establishing and "transmitting" the cultural values of Old Town and its African American community, despite the racially charged Temperance Movement stories in newspapers that would sometimes attempt to discredit his business.

Sykes also played a role in the political life of Decatur. Not surprisingly for African Americans in the post-war South, he was a Republican, distinguishing his political views from those of his father and former enslaver.[37] Not surprisingly, for politically active African Americans in the post-war South, his activism was met with bigotry. In a letter to the editor of the *Alabama Enquirer,* a commentator argued that he "was all for political conventions," referring to a meeting attended by Sol Sykes, "but never with a negro" and advised fellow readers that they "may profit by keeping out from the dusky brethren here after."[38]

Sykes's saloon prospered, narrowly avoiding damage in a fire that devasted Old Town's business district.[39] He became, by the turn of the century, "one of the wealthiest negroes in North Alabama."[40] He would "quit the saloon business" following his baptism. On an October Sunday in 1900, he joined two of his brothers and a thousand other men and women, proceeding to the Tennessee River near Bank Street, and received the sacrament from Elder Robinson, pastor of the Baptist Church.[41] Solomon Sykes had been preparing for a change in career. He had purchased land and begun construction of a "three-story" building on Bank Street. Initially, Sykes shared the property with a jewelry store, his funeral home occupying two of the three stories.[42] Construction on the business offices was finished in mid-January 1901.[43]

The families that come together today to watch their children play ball at Matthews Field and those who join in the Freedom Pioneers historic tours of Old Town gather in rituals of community and of remembrance. Baseball and Civil Rights form the heart of contemporary celebrations of African American culture in Old Town Decatur. It is fitting then that Frank "Doc" Sykes and his family feature in the tours of the city—they are part of its history and of its spiritual geography. It was in Old Town that Frank Sykes learned to read and write, and it was there that he learned to play baseball. It was there, too, where he learned pride, courage, and perseverance. Nurtured by his father and his mother, both at one time considered the property of another; sustained by his brothers and sisters and by his neighbors, Frank Sykes became a person who could maintain his dignity and conduct himself honorably in the face of bigotry and hatred. In just the way he and his family shaped Old Town, the African American community there shaped who he became. Frank Sykes would leave Old Town to study at Atlanta Baptist College and later Howard University, but, in many ways, he never left the community.

CHAPTER 4

A LIVING FORCE

FRANK SYKES AT ATLANTA BAPTIST COLLEGE (MOREHOUSE COLLEGE) AND HOWARD UNIVERSITY

For the African American community, 1910 proved to be an eventful and important year. In New York, W. E. B. Du Bois, at the head of a "conference on the status of colored people," founded the National Association for the Advancement of Colored People (NAACP). The NAACP set forward its goals that included cooperation with "all agencies working for the uplift of" African Americans; the "discovery and redress of cases of injustice"; and the "systematic study of the present conditions among colored people." The NAACP resolved to achieve these ends in part by "holding mass meetings and conferences," publishing pamphlets and articles in newspapers and magazines, and through a regular journal titled *The Crisis*.[1] The editors of *The Crisis* explained that they "believe that this [1910] is a critical time in the history of the advancement of men." They saw a conflict and a crisis erupting in the country. The battle was between "tolerance, reason, and forbearance" and "bigotry and prejudice." The editors explained that the latter must not "succeed in pushing back and possibly overwhelming a deserving and rising class of colored people."[2]

Frank Sykes was one of that rising class. For him, 1910 also proved to be an eventful and important year. He moved away from Old Town and left his family home. He began what became an eight-year educational journey that took him to Atlanta and then to Washington, DC. He first studied at Atlanta Baptist College (Morehouse College) for two years and then moved on to Howard University. He started his journey as a young man, just eighteen years old, and ended it as a doctor of dental surgery from one of the leading universities in the United States.

He became a product of what are now known as historically black colleges and universities (HBCUs). Their history is an important part of his story, and understanding what Atlanta Baptist College and Howard were when he enrolled can tell us a great deal about the man he became. The ideals of "Black colleges," as they were then known, involved imbuing in their graduates physical, moral, and spiritual courage as well as intellectual and professional development. The man who testified at the Scottsboro Boys trials and the man who advocated for equal pay with the Black Sox was nurtured by his family and by the African American community in Old Town. Howard and Atlanta Baptist College further refined and developed that young man.

Sykes undoubtedly came across that first issue of *The Crisis*, published toward the end of his first semester in Atlanta. Reading the articles and notes, he would have found a resonance with his experiences of segregation in Decatur. He would have discovered that white-controlled municipal governments in Baltimore, St. Louis, Kansas City, and Richmond were discussing enshrining housing segregation into law.[3] He would have also been reminded of his good fortune in growing up in a community that offered primary and secondary education to African Americans. *The Crisis* detailed how half of young African Americans in Atlanta, where he was studying, did not attend school. He would have read about the city of Chattanooga, which had "refused to take steps towards establishing a Negro normal school," and he would have read about the "white boys" in Chicago, who "tried to get rid of the Negro pupils." Frank Sykes would have also read about the outpouring of generosity to Black colleges. Morris Brown, a neighboring HBCU in Atlanta, recently received a bequest for $25,000—raised from the African American community where only half of its youth went to school. *The Crisis* also detailed a $250,000 bequest to Hampton and $400,000 to Tuskegee.[4] Frank Sykes certainly knew how fortunate he was and appreciated both his personal and the African American community's circumstances.

Atlanta Baptist College

On Sunday, June 19, 1910, *The Atlanta Journal-Constitution* published a poem titled "The Prisoner at the Bar" by Benjamin Griffith Brawley. The poem contrasts two figures, one real and one ephemeral. The first stands, "Waiting for the pleasure of the court;" he will be sentenced for a crime. He is "bewildered" and "dazed." He is described as "one more black boy accused of thievery." The other figure is an imagined boy who knows "Shakespeare" and

"Isaac Newton." The poem turns abruptly to the first boy, considering "what means the music of the spheres to him" and "his soul's thousand vague desires."[5] Brawley, in the first stanza, plays on the meaning of "pleasure." In the context of a court of law, "pleasure" suggests submission to the will of a legal authority. The poem reinforces the meaning. A "black boy" is submissive to a system where conviction is certain. Another meaning of "pleasure" suggests that not just the judge but also the "court," the justice system, enjoys and takes pleasure in the young man's submissive predicament and posture.

Frank Sykes would fight against that system when he testified before the court advocating on behalf of the Scottsboro Boys. Sykes also knew of the other figure in the poem, the ephemeral young man who contemplates "Shakespeare," "Newton," and "the music of the spheres." He himself studied literature, science, and philosophy at Atlanta Baptist College, which is "second to none in the South for preparing young men for literary work."[6] The poem's author also knew of those young men. Benjamin Griffith Brawley was an English professor at Atlanta Baptist College. Though the young Frank Sykes did not take any classes with him, Brawley played an important role in his life.

Atlanta Baptist College, renamed Morehouse College shortly after Frank Sykes left to study dentistry at Howard University, is a historically black college. Atlanta Baptist College was founded in 1867 by Baptist ministers William Jefferson White, Edmund Turney, and Richard C. Coulter, a formerly enslaved man. Known then as the "Augusta Institute,"[7] it opened under threats by the Ku Klux Klan.[8] In 1879, the Institute moved to Atlanta and became the Atlanta Baptist Seminary. Its name later changed from "seminary" to "college" to encourage students seeking careers in addition to ministry. Students enrolled in a set curriculum that included "algebra, geometry, physiology, botany, the natural sciences, rhetoric, Latin, and New Testament Greek."[9] With its focus on the liberal arts, the college followed the spirit of W. E. B. Du Bois as opposed to Booker T. Washington's Tuskegee Institute, which focused on agricultural and technical education. Du Bois felt that "education and work are the levers to uplift a people. Work alone will not do it unless inspired by the right ideals and guided by intelligence. Education must not simply teach work—it must teach life."[10] Despite their differing emphases, the Black colleges founded in the decades after the Civil War shared a common mission.

Historically black colleges and universities throughout the nation and particularly in the South were established, like Augusta Institute (now Morehouse College), despite the threat of violence. For African Americans, the colleges "reflected the ex-slaves intent to restructure and control their lives." For the former enslavers and their supporters, their "civilization depended much if not more, on the containment and repression of literate culture among its enslaved population."[11] Brawley reflects the struggle between the two forces in his poem "Prisoner at the Bar," and Frank Sykes's life and those of fellow African Americans in the period also reflect this struggle.

The HBCUs also served another purpose, what Jelani Favors in *Shelter in a Time of Storm* calls "an unwritten *second* curriculum." She speaks of the "bond between teacher and student," which functions as a "pedagogy of hope grounded in idealism, race consciousness, and cultural nationalism."[12] Du Bois's and Washington's curricular models share common bonds founded in resistance to violence and historical repression, and also manifest the bonds found in the sense of community formed on campuses, even those as varied as Tuskegee and Atlanta Baptist College. The president of Atlanta Baptist College during Frank Sykes's time at the school, John C. Hope, wrote that his college was "a center of racial and community uplift."[13]

Frank Sykes joined that community in the fall of 1910. He likely traveled the two hundred miles by train. Arriving at the station, he would have discovered, just west "beyond the terminal," an African American educational community "little known or heeded by the white community."[14] The campus, occupying about twelve and a half acres, was situated on a hill that "overlook[ed] the city and surrounding county." About five acres were "cultivated as a school garden," and over two hundred trees lined pathways across campus and between school buildings. There were six buildings on campus: a barn, a laundry building, the president's house, a dormitory, and two classroom buildings.[15] The president's residence, the classroom buildings, and the dormitory were all erected within a few years of Frank Sykes's arrival.

Sale Hall, home to the gym and chapel, as well as the Divinity School and mechanical engineering lab, had been partially funded by "the Negro People of the South." They raised $5,000 for the building. Andrew Carnegie contributed $10,000. Quarles Hall had a large first-floor entrance hall with memorials to the college's former presidents. Students passed through the entrance hall for large lecture classes and for smaller rooms reserved for discussion.

The third floor contained the science lecture rooms and labs.[16]

Atlanta Baptist College offered a rich extracurricular life for its students. There was a newspaper, *The Athenaeum*, published monthly; an orchestra; and a glee club.[17] *The Atlanta Constitution* informed its readers that the glee club would be singing "plantation melodies" in concert. In the column adjacent to that announcement, the paper mentioned that the "Marist Cadets," students from an all-white school, would be performing a "Minstrel Show" in blackface.[18] Atlanta Baptist College also offered intercollegiate athletics in football and baseball.

The baseball team was part of a four-team league that included Atlanta University, Morris Brown College, and Clark University. Atlanta Baptist College also played against other regional HBCUs, including Tuskegee.[19] Frank Sykes pitched for Atlanta Baptist College for two seasons.[20] The only surviving mention of Sykes comes from a short notice in *The Atlanta Constitution*, stating that Sykes will be "pitching for Atlanta Baptist College against Clark University."[21] Years later, Doc Sykes told John Holway that he pitched against the great Negro League pitcher, Dick "Cannonball" Redding in Atlanta.[22] Redding went on to join the New York Lincoln Giants in April 1911. The only time during which Sykes and Redding would have played in Atlanta was in March 1911; on March 22, Redding's team, the Atlanta Dephins, played an exhibition game against Atlanta Baptist College.[23] It is likely this is when Redding faced Sykes during the spring semester of Sykes's freshman year. Within a few years, Frank Sykes would also pitch for the Lincoln Giants.

Atlanta Baptist College baseball team (1912). Sykes sits in the top row, fourth from the right.

As Frank Sykes finished his sophomore year in the spring of 1912, the college's new dean, Benjamin Brawley, asked to speak with him. Brawley had returned to Atlanta after two years as a professor and administrator at Howard University. Brawley urged the young Sykes to go to Howard University to study dentistry and wrote him a letter of recommendation.[24] Admittance to medical or dental school after two years of college, conditional on the successful completion of certain courses and on a letter of recommendation, was standard in the field at the time. The American Medical Association and the National Association of Dental Faculties had recently instituted nationwide changes for admittance to doctoral programs.[25] Georgetown University, for example, also offered admission to medical school with two years of undergraduate work and a recommendation.[26]

Brawley's letter and advice changed Frank Sykes's life. Indeed, Benjamin Brawley changed many young men's lives. Writing in *Phylon*, John W. Parker memorialized him thus: "He spent his life in the struggle to give Negro people the widest education . . . and to set no limit on their cultural advancement."[27] In his book, *The Negro in Literature and Art in the United States*, Brawley wrote of the "heart" of the African American community: it "speaks of the lash, of the child torn from its mother's bosom, of the dead body riddled with bullets and singing all night from . . . the roadside."[28] Brawley understood what happens to young Black men in America and particularly in the South. Frank Sykes was one of many Brawley nurtured and for whom he took an active role to prevent them from standing at the "pleasure of the court."

Howard University

On May 26, 1909, United States President William Howard Taft gave the commencement address at Howard University. His presence was an indication of the prestigious and elite nature of what became Frank Sykes's home three years later. In his 1909 commencement address, Taft mentioned other Black colleges, lamenting their lack of funding and regretting that the states did not allocate more. He said that the federal government, at least in the District of Columbia as it is under federal control, can "assume the obligation and maintenance of a first-class University for the education of colored men." Taft framed the obligation as a "debt owned by the people of the United States." Taft then characterized that debt in moral and spiritual terms, saying "that God has put [that debt] upon the people of the United States." For Taft, funding for Howard University was reparations: it was "the partial payment of a debt—only partial—to a race to which the government and people of the United States are eternally indebted. They brought that race into this country against its will. They planted it here irretrievably. They first put it in bondage and then kept it in the ignorance that that bondage seemed to make necessary. . . . Then they freed it and put upon it the responsibilities of citizenship."[29] The president spoke aloud and in a public forum about his views on reparations and funding for what would become HBCUs. For Frank Sykes, coming from Alabama and Georgia, it must have seemed an alternate world, one in which a government leader acknowledges the sins of that government against African Americans and takes action to make reparations for those sins.

When Frank Sykes arrived at Howard University for the fall semester in 1912, he could not help being impressed with the campus. It "was situated on a high plateau overlooking the entire city of Washington and practically surrounded on all sides by parks." The city's "Reservoir Lake" bordered the "campus on the East," and Frank Sykes had a clear view beyond the reservoir of Griffith Stadium, home to the Washington Senators. Howard was a landscape of "beautiful shade trees" that lined "the long avenues." The main campus building was "considered one of the best of its kind in the country." It sat 185 feet above the Potomac River and was visible "to all sections of the city." Senators and representatives from the South, their Northern and Western allies, and bigots in and out of government must have found its presence—and the constant reminder of the dignity of African Americans—abhorrent.

However, the prominence of Howard University would be, both literally and metaphorically, a manifestation of John Winthrop's promise of "a city upon a hill." For African Americans, it was their birthright, despite bigotry and prejudice.

Frank Sykes also found an abundance of newly constructed buildings on the campus. The Carnegie Library was a model for universities nationwide. The new medical building was "well supplied" with state-of-the-art labs and lecture halls. They were "modern and well equipped." Students could serve the equivalent of a residency at a hospital near campus. The dental school was experiencing rapid growth. Founded in 1868, it grew from eight graduates in 1905 to more than forty in 1916.[30] The intellectual climate of the school sought a balance between the educational philosophies of Booker T. Washington and W. E. B. Du Bois. Washington served on Howard's Board of Trustees, and his influence was "instrumental" in the construction of the "new Medical and Science buildings."[31]

The university also welcomed a new president during the fall 1912 semester. Stephan Morrell Newman spoke of the value of the imagination as a transformative power. Clearly influenced by the writings of Samuel Taylor Coleridge, Stephen Morrell Newman saw the imagination both as a spiritual force and a call to action. He spoke of the power of the "imaginative faculty" as "common to all peoples, but [it] becomes a living force only when accompanied by a training that will bring . . . [it] in touch with the problems that it must meet and solve." Acknowledging how African Americans had been denied access to education, he stated that they, "in common with the other peoples of the earth, [are] endowed with this imaginative faculty. The race should have every opportunity for its development."[32]

Frank Sykes entered a world that was alive with promise and opportunities, which he embraced. In addition to pursuing a rigorous academic and professional course, he played on the basketball and baseball teams. In baseball, he showed the promise that would manifest itself as the pitcher who no-hit the Bacharach Giants in 1922.

In May 1914, he pitched for Howard in an exhibition game against the Brooklyn Royal Giants, a professional African American (pre-Negro League) team. The *Washington Herald* described his performance as "masterful." He struck out eight of the best hitters in baseball. Howard lost the game, but Sykes pitched the entire extra-inning affair (eleven innings total). He was clearly nervous, perhaps struggling with a new pitch, his trademark spitball. He hit three batters and threw three wild pitches.[33]

Later that season, he demonstrated greater command of his pitches, throwing a two-hit shutout against Lincoln University and a one-hitter against a local semipro team.[34] In subsequent seasons, he became a fixture in Howard's rotation, holding "batters at his mercy" and keeping "them eating out of his hand."[35] His accomplishments on the mound attracted the attention of major African American professional and semiprofessional teams. Howard University not only trained him for a career as a practicing dentist—it showcased his talents as a major league-caliber baseball player.

Howard University basketball team (1916). Frank Sykes stands at the far right of the photo.

President Taft returned to Howard University less than a year after his rousing commencement address. In March 1910, he spoke at the dedication of the university's Carnegie Library. Taft's remarks were brief and, by comparison to his earlier address, uninspiring. He noted that the library "will add to the efficiency of the education both of those who study in the academic departments and of those who study in professional departments." In his final, short closing, he uses the word "colored" five times.[36] President Taft had a troubling Civil Rights record, but he had moments of insight into and empathy for African Americans. In an address in 1912 to Howard University undergraduates and professional students, Taft "condemned lynching," calling it "cowardly murder" and advocating that "the man that pulls the rope should hang by the rope." [37, 38]

Despite his moments of outrage against lynching and for African American education as a form of reparations, Taft had a troubled Civil Rights history. In fact, his 1912 speech on lynching, as meaningful as it was, attracted a "fair audience," but "many of the most prominent colored residents of the District of Columbia were absent," indicating their anger and frustration with Taft and his policies on race. After he was introduced, he was "feebly applauded." *The Afro* wrote that the president "made no reference to his policy of excluding colored men from high political office in the South." Moreover, *The Afro* pointed out that his comments on lynching are "somewhat late" and that he had not urged "Congress to enact legislation against it."[39]

Taft was primarily a politician, and advocating for African Americans' human rights was secondary to his bid to win votes and reelection. Woodrow Wilson was already emerging as the favorite in the 1912 election. There were rumblings, which proved prescient, that Teddy Roosevelt would run as a third-party progressive candidate. Taft wanted to present himself as a compromise between Wilson and Roosevelt. Ultimately, he would fail to win reelection and, in the end, also fail to live up to the moral obligations he spoke of in his commencement address in 1909.

After Taft's remarks, Rev. Wilbur Patterson Thirkield, Howard University's president, stood to speak. He was born into an abolitionist family in Ohio and had been a lifelong advocate for African American rights. He had given his main address before Taft's remarks, and Thirkield was scheduled to conclude the ceremony with a brief thank-you to Taft, Andrew Carnegie, and the other dignitaries in attendance. Thirkield did express appreciation but then spoke of the library and the university as serving the "cause of liberal culture," noticeably leaving out the word "colored." He then spoke of the "nearly thirteen hundred students, representing thirty-five states and eleven countries." Thirkield made it clear to Taft and others in attendance that Howard University was a place for African American men and women to come for an education, but that it was also a leading national and international university. Thirkield then spoke of his ambition that Howard's graduates be "moral, industrial, and spiritual leaders of the people," regardless of race.[40]

Frank Sykes proved himself to be one of those leaders, offering moral and spiritual guidance and physical courage in his testimony for and actions on behalf of the Scottsboro Boys, as well as being a successful dentist and baseball player. Sykes and the country changed significantly during the eight years after he left his home and the Old Town community in Decatur, Alabama. The nation became embroiled in the First World War. The June 1918 issue of *The Crisis* dedicated itself to the "Negro Soldier." The African American community continued to suffer lynchings, bigotry, and segregation. However, the years since 1910 had also seen a growth in the African American professional class and organized resistance to oppression.

The teenaged Frank Sykes perhaps read, in the inaugural issue of *The Crisis,* a story about the emerging and prosperous African American community on Druid Hill Avenue in Baltimore as an example of what *The Crisis* characterized as an "inevitable step forward in anti-Negro prejudice."[41] Howard Young, a fellow Howard alumnus, worked as a pharmacist and owned his own business on Druid Hill Avenue. He was active in the NAACP and in efforts to resist the city's segregation laws and discriminatory practices. Within a few years, Dr. Frank Sykes would become a member of that community and Howard Young's neighbor.

CHAPTER 5

THE GRANDEST TIME

FRANK SYKES STARTS HIS PROFESSIONAL BASEBALL CAREER

Like many college students, Frank Sykes had to work during breaks between terms to help pay for his education and for his spending money for the school year. Unlike many students, he "paid his dental tuition while playing" ball.[1] He had not yet earned his doctorate and consequent moniker, "Doc," but his teammates and the newspapers called him "Schoolboy Sykes."[2] He would play for several different teams—not an unusual circumstance for African American ballplayers at that time. As Robert Peterson notes in *Only the Ball Was White*, "Player contracts were non-existent, or at best informal agreements. As a result, there was a great deal of shifting from team to team. . . . Because of this fluidity, the *Chicago Defender* [and other sources] always referred to black teams as semipro, even when they were playing two-hundred games a year."[3] Evidence suggests that he would pitch on weekends in May and September and would join teams for all games in June, July, and August. His work would take him as far west as Chicago and St. Louis, into New England, and along the Atlantic Seaboard into the South. He would have had to suffer the same conditions as his teammates. Travel was not comfortable by bus or train—and he would have to endure prejudice and discrimination—but he formed bonds with his teammates and developed both as a pitcher and as a person.

1914

In 1914, Frank Sykes, just twenty-two years old, went from pitching for Howard University to his summer job, pitching in the African American professional and semiprofessional circuit. Available records indicate that he threw in nineteen games for two teams, the Lincoln Giants and the Brooklyn Royal Giants. His combined record was eight wins against six losses. In the other five games, he either appeared as a reliever or as a starting pitcher but left those games without a decision. He would pitch against white, semipro teams; semipro African American teams; and against Rube Foster's Chicago American Giants, among the elite, professional African American teams in the nation. He acquitted himself well, given that it was his first year in pro baseball. His season started after Howard University's academic year and collegiate baseball season ended. He pitched his first game in May for the Lincoln Giants. His last game for Lincoln would come seven weeks later when he took the mound against the Brooklyn Royal Giants. He appeared in five games, with a record of two wins and two losses. It's likely he pitched in others, but the available records only list the five.

The Lincoln Giants were founded in New York in 1911 by brothers Edward and Roderick "Jess" McMahon. They hired Sol White, the man who had built the Philadelphia Giants into an elite franchise and perennial contender and champion; White also wrote *Sol White's Official Baseball Guide* (1907), the indispensable first history of the African American game. In 1910, White managed the Brooklyn Royal Giants, but White had a falling-out with Nat Strong, the Royal Giants' owner, who had pulled the Royal Giants from their moorings in Brooklyn and turned them into a traveling team. For Lincoln, White raided his old team, the Philadelphia Giants, and the players who had been with him in Philadelphia but had left for the Chicago American Giants. The result was not simply a competitive squad but "a major force."[4] The *Brooklyn Daily Eagle* reported that White and the "McMahon Brothers, well known promoters of sporting events in New York, will have . . . one of the strongest aggregations of colored ballplayers ever gotten together."[5] They included Louis Santop, Dick "Cannonball" Redding, and John Henry Lloyd. Before the 1914 season, Lloyd and Smokey Joe Williams, the future Hall of Fame pitcher, left Lincoln to play for Rube Foster's American Giants in Chicago.[6] Nonetheless, Sykes joined a team with an albeit short but rich and winning tradition.

The newspapers announced his arrival: "Sykes, the star pitcher of Howard University, hurled his first game for the Lincoln Giants on Sunday," May 29.[7] He allowed four runs on seven hits, and the Giants would lose. There are no records for Sykes until he's listed as a starter for a Fourth of July game, when he allowed six runs in a seven-to-six loss to the Brooklyn Royal Giants.[8] He would walk two batters and strike out one, allowing seven hits in three innings of work.[9] His first recorded professional victory came against Riverhead, a white semipro team. He pitched a complete game, allowing two runs on eight hits, with two walks and five strikeouts. He also had a hit and scored a run in support of his own effort.[10] He pitched even better in his next start against Tarrytown, striking out six and allowing one walk and seven hits in an eight-to-one victory. He also hit a batter.[11] He was gaining his footing at the professional level. The *Atlantic City Gazette Review* announced that he was the scheduled starter for a July 18 game against the Brooklyn Royal Giants. Although no records survive that detail his performance, Frank Sykes must have been impressive because his next recorded start would be for the Royal Giants.

Sykes may have left the Lincoln Giants because of an ownership dispute and the resulting schism. The McMahon brothers "left the team to found a rival club, the Lincoln Stars, while Jim Keenan took over the Giants."[12] The split was acrimonious. The Lincoln Giants placed advertisements stating that they were, "The Colored Champions of the World," and that they have "positively no connection with the Lincoln Stars."[13] In interviews, the Giants' manager stressed that his team is "not the Lincoln Stars, but the real Giants."[14] The Stars, for their part, proclaimed that they were "one of the fastest and strongest traveling teams in the country."[15] For a young Frank Sykes, in an era that lacked exclusive contracts, a move to the Royal Giants may have seemed the best option rather than choosing a side in the Lincoln controversy.

The Brooklyn Royal Giants, run by Nat Strong, had just reorganized and started their season in July.[16] The team was founded in 1904 by John W. Connor, owner of the "Royal Café on Myrtle Avenue." Connor was "an all-around athlete" and "a baseball player of no mean ability." He was also one of Brooklyn's "leading-colored citizens both socially and politically."[17] To form his club, Connor partnered with James E. Boone, who was owner-general manager of the "Colored Niantics."[18] Boone had formed his team in 1902 and, in 1903, had won the "colored championship of Brooklyn." He had the aspiration to compete on the national level and talked about fielding a club that could be competitive with the Philadelphia Giants and the Cuban Giants.[19] Boone likely sought Connor's financial resources to acquire the players to make the team a national force. Their partnership would last only a year. Strong wrestled control of the Royal Giants from Connor. In February 1905, Boone resigned, and Nat Strong became the Royal Giants' business manager.[20] Strong, a white man, had a reputation as an abrasive and even bigoted man. John Connor publicly accused him of racism.[21] Nat Strong was likely prejudiced. He may have seen the Royal Giants as a financial investment only. To make the most money from his investment, he sought out the most talented African American ballplayers, and in July 1914, he convinced Frank Sykes to leave the Lincoln Giants and pitch for the Brooklyn Royal Giants.

Frank Sykes pitched in fourteen games for the Royal Giants in 1914; he played right field in another, getting a hit and scoring a run in that game.[22] In August, he pitched well, earning five wins against a single loss (and two appearances without a decision). His only loss that month came in the first game he pitched for Brooklyn. Sykes allowed one run on three hits. He struck out nine and walked just one batter in a complete-game loss. The Atlantic

City pitcher shut out the Royal Giants. *The Press of Atlantic City* called it a "Great Exhibition," telling readers that there "never was a prettier game." Sykes also singled and stole a base in his debut. It was an auspicious start with his new team.[23] His next appearance was in relief in a twelve-to-four loss to the Bushwicks, a semipro team. He pitched six and two-thirds innings, allowing four runs, four hits, and a walk. He also hit a batter but had three strikeouts.[24] Sykes would earn a victory in his next start against the Cliftons, another semipro team, before making two consecutive appearances against the Bushwicks.[25] The Royal Giants would win both, although Sykes would have a no decision in the first game. In the first game, he "pitched excellently for three innings" but left with two outs in the fourth inning after allowing five hits.[26] In the next game, he would be the winning pitcher, scattering eight hits in an eleven-to-four win against the Bushwicks.[27] He would close out the month with three consecutive victories over teams from Ashbury Park, Disston, and Atlantic City.[28] The summer was over, and Howard University's fall semester was about to begin. Frank Sykes had made an impressive start in professional baseball, but his season was not over.

Brooklyn Royal Giants baseball team (1916). Sykes stands at the far left.

He continued to pitch for the Royal Giants in September and early October while simultaneously taking classes at Howard. His record reflects the difficulties such a workload must have taken on him. The competition was stronger as well, with games against the Chicago American Giants and the Philadelphia Giants. He would pitch in five games—about one each week—and would win only one game against Camden City while losing three.[29] His losses would be to the Bushwicks and the Chicago American Giants.[30] His best game, including his one win, came when he faced Chicago for the second time. The *Chicago Tribune* mentioned that "Sykes worked well," striking out five in a three-to-two complete-game loss.[31] He could return to his academic life, satisfied that he had pitched well but also understanding the difficulties of balancing both professions.

It was a lesson that would serve him well in the coming years as he balanced his careers as a dentist and as a baseball player.

1915

In 1915, Frank Sykes pitched for three teams and had a combined record of nineteen wins against five losses. While pitching for the Philadelphia Giants, Sykes recorded three wins and one loss. He had fifteen wins and four losses for the Lincoln Stars and one win for the Lincoln Giants. In just his second year in professional baseball, Sykes showed his maturity and his developing skills. White semipro teams comprised the bulk of his competition, but he also pitched against major-league-caliber teams, such as the Almendares, from the Cuban professional league; the Chicago American Giants; the Cubans; and Bender's All-Stars, a collection of white-professional players organized by Chief Bender, a future Hall of Fame pitcher who had just finished the season for the Baltimore Terrapins of the Federal League. Importantly, Sykes was enrolled in dental school and had to work around his academic schedule. He was still a young man, shouldering professional duties against older, more seasoned, and very skilled semipro and major-league-caliber competition.

Other teams and opposing fans would not hesitate to remind him of his relative lack of experience, attempting to rattle him. In August, just a few weeks before he would return to school, the Lincoln Stars engaged Rube Foster's Chicago American Giants in what was arranged to be a championship series between the two teams, representing the best of the Eastern African American teams,

Lincoln, and the Western champions, the American Giants. Frank Young, writing in the *Chicago Defender,* describes the scene: For the opening game in Chicago, "there was a big band. . . . It paraded up and down the streets." The "crowds began to storm the box office, the boxes began to fill, the players began to get in action, the bell rang for the New York team to take the field to practice." The atmosphere was sufficient to test even veteran players, and the Lincoln Stars' starting pitcher was met "with an avalanche of blows" from a Chicago starting lineup that included future Hall of Famers Pete Hill and John Henry "Pop" Lloyd. As Harvey walked toward the dugout, the band, which had marched into the stadium and positioned itself near the Lincoln dugout, played "When You're a Long, Long Way from Home." The crowd was cheering in response to the early lead and to the band's taunting. At that moment, Frank Sykes walked to the mound. He would pitch the remainder of the game for the Stars. He did well.

Frank Young observed that "Sykes was going good, but the tension was high and the errors [7] were too numerous behind him." On the mound, Sykes responded better than his veteran teammates to the atmosphere in Chicago. At the plate, he dismissed any notion that he could be rattled. When he "came to bat in the fifth inning wearing a blue sweater . . . a Howard University sweater. The band played 'Memphis Blues.' Sykes singled sharply." The final line of the first stanza of "Memphis Blues" reads, "I couldn't spend a dime and had the grandest time."[32] In spite of the difficulties he faced, Frank Sykes did indeed have the "grandest time"—while the tensions of the game disturbed more experienced players, he kept his composure.

The championship games between the Lincoln Stars and the Chicago American Giants took place in August. Sykes began the season as a “star pitcher of the Philadelphia Giants.”[33] The team was not, of course, Sol White’s Giants but rather one of several nationwide picking up the name. Philadelphia had teams known as the South Philadelphia Giants, the North Philadelphia Giants, the East Philadelphia Giants, and the West Philadelphia Giants. Sykes’s Giants team had been founded in 1913. The on-field manager of the team in 1915 was its catcher, Jimmy Fuller, who had played for the Cuban Giants the year before. A. C. Baxter was their business manager. He had also played for the Cuban Giants. Sykes’s teammates were either young players whose careers would last a year or two or veterans of various African American semipro teams at the end of their careers. There were exceptions. Charlie Bradford, a pitcher, would play in the Eastern Colored League for the New York Lincoln Giants in the late 1920s, and Louis Miller, the third baseman, would be Sykes’s teammate with the Baltimore Black Sox in the early ’20s.[34] In the three games against local semipro clubs that Sykes played for the Giants in May, he pitched to an ERA of 1.33 and a WHIP of .852. He walked eight batters in twenty-seven innings and recorded twenty strikeouts.[35] At the end of that month, Sykes left the Giants for more familiar territory. He did return to Philadelphia for a game in June, losing badly to the Lincoln Giants, twelve to two.[36]

Apart from one game in September—which he pitched for the Lincoln Giants in a seven-to-one win over Harrisburg—Sykes played for the Lincoln Stars.[37] There are several reasons why Sykes decided to pitch for Philadelphia in May. The team’s schedule might have been best suited to his academic schedule. They could have offered him more money than other teams. However, there are clues that suggest another possibility. He may have been waiting for an offer from Nat Strong and the Brooklyn Royal Giants, and, in early June, he received word that Brooklyn "will not take the field this season."[38] At that point, he could have made the decision to return to the Stars. The acrimony between the Stars and the Giants appears to have cooled somewhat, and the rosters stabilized enough for Sykes to feel comfortable going back to his old club. The rival parties seemed to have arrived at an uneasy truce, with the McMahons controlling the Stars and Jim Keenan keeping the Giants.[39] Even still, the McMahons, in advertisements for the Stars, declared the team the "Colored Champions of the World,"[40] suggesting that, although the acrimony may have abated, the spirit that inspired the rivalry lingered.

While pitching for the Stars against semipro and local African American teams, Sykes "held" them "at his mercy."[41] Even in his few losses, he pitched well, striking out sixteen batters while losing to the Long Branch Cubans by three to two.[42] Earlier that year, he shut out the Cubans on four hits.[43] Against top-rate, professional competition, Sykes performed well. His work included games against the Chicago American Giants but also against the Indianapolis ABCs and the Almendares Scorpions of the Cuban League. He would earn the win in the Stars five-to-two victory over the ABCs, but he needed help: "Sykes, the lanky star of Howard University, was removed in the sixth when he walked two men and when he had been touched up for two singles and a double."[44] Against the visiting Cuban team, Sykes shut them out, allowing four hits in the Stars' four-to-zero win.[45]

Frank Sykes's most impressive performance of 1915 came in a losing effort. He started a game in the championship series against the Chicago American Giants, in which the band had earlier taunted him about his sweater when he entered the game in relief. He would pitch twelve innings, allowing two runs, scattering eleven hits, striking out four, and offering three walks.[46] The game became the stuff of legend: "Folks played the game over and over." Years later, Frank Young recalled "that hot Sunday in August." The pitchers "hooked up in a pitching duel. For 11 innings they sweated and fumed." In the bottom of the twelfth inning, Sykes walked Pete Hill. He moved to second on a sacrifice bunt. "The crowd pulled for Lloyd to hit, but Sykes walked him purposely." The runners advanced on a grounder to Sykes. He threw to first for the sure out. With two outs, Leroy Grant "poked a single over second and Hill scored."[47] Frank Sykes held his own for eleven innings against Rube Foster's Chicago American Giants. His near victory cemented his reputation in the eyes of African American baseball fans and management. He would return to Howard University to continue his studies, but his place in professional, pre-Negro League ball was secure. The game would wait for him to return next season.

In his first two years in professional baseball, "Schoolboy" Sykes established a reputation as a good, if not great, pitcher. He was cool and level-headed in times of stress. He would play with and against men like Rube Foster and Pete Hill, both of whom would be enshrined in Cooperstown. Sykes would also meet players about whom we know very little and whose accomplishments, had they been white, would be legendary. In part, he shared their fate. He would be in his prime as a player in the years before the establishment of the recognized Negro Leagues. Consequently, very few of his accomplishments are part of the official major league record book, but they were nonetheless impressive. Like many of the men who performed at a very high level in African American professional ball in the first decades of the twentieth century, he labored in the wilderness. Importantly, his work at that time was well-known and astonishingly well-documented. Readers of both the mainstream press and the African American press could read about his exploits and follow his career. His name appears in box scores and in news accounts in papers from prominent cities like New York, Brooklyn, and Chicago, to lesser-known papers in the South and West. In the coming years, he would play for more established teams and better-known franchises, like Hilldale and Baltimore. He would serve time in the military, finish his degree, and become "Doc" Sykes.

CHAPTER 6

"SCHOOLBOY" SYKES HELD THEM "IN THE HOLLOW OF HIS HAND"

Frank Sykes had made enough of an impression in 1915 that *The New York Age* announced his arrival in its June 1, 1916 edition: "Sykes, a student at Howard University who pitched for the Lincoln Giants during his vacation, arrived in the city Saturday [May 29]"[1] to play baseball. His appearance was worthy of a story in the sports pages, but other news dominated the headlines. It was becoming increasingly apparent that the United States would enter the First World War, and the front-page story in *The New York Age* discussed the army's troop buildup and confronted issues of race and service. Under the headline "War Department and Enlistment," the paper addressed two issues. The first involved a decision by the war department "against the designation of anymore Negro Regiments." The second involved segregation in the military. Acknowledging that "Army officers as a rule believe, in the best interests of the service, whites and Negroes should be placed in separate regiments." However, the story also noted that "there are many white Army officers on record who believe it would be to the best interests of the service to mix the races and have no regiments for any particular race."[2] Racism and segregation, the same issues Frank Sykes faced in baseball, confronted the nation at a time when the country was preparing for war. Frank Sykes would confront those issues over the next few years. He would excel as a pitcher for the Lincoln Giants, the Brooklyn Royal Giants, and Hilldale. He would also serve his country.

1916

For Frank Sykes, 1916 was a tale of two seasons. He had a respectable overall record of nine wins against five losses, but in September and October, pitching for the Royal Giants, he won five games, losing only once. Pitching for the Lincoln Stars in June, July, and August, his record was four wins and four losses.[3] The difference in Sykes's performance is likely a result of pitching for a better team. The Lincoln Stars, after the 1915 season, lost six players from their starting lineup. They added a nineteen-year-old, Oscar Charleston, who performed spectacularly. He played center field and batted .393.[4] His bat, on paper, compensated for the loss of John Henry Lloyd, who had played second base, and batted .397 in 1915. Lloyd left Lincoln to play for Foster's Chicago American Giants. Nonetheless, the Lincoln Stars were only a shadow of the team they had been the year before. In 1915, their record was twenty-four wins and fifteen losses. Lloyd had been their manager for twenty-one of those wins. Without him at the helm, they were a .500 ballclub.[5] The Stars relied on their reputation for favorable coverage. The *Chicago Defender* ran a headline and a team photo, declaring them "Eastern Champions" and captioning the photo with the comment that they were "McMahon's Classy Ballclub." Bill Pettus was the team's manager and first baseman. He batted .376 that year, but according to the papers, it was McMahon's team.[6] Despite the headline, the 1916 Stars felt the loss—not just of Lloyd's on-field performance but also of his leadership. They were not the team they had been a year before. Conversely, the Royal Giants had a new manager in 1916 and played a full season, something they had not done for years. They scoured the nation for players: "Charles Babcock Earl, manager of the reconstructed Brooklyn Royal Giants, returned to town yesterday from the West, where he has been for several weeks on a still hunt for ball players."[7] Under Earl, they finished the 1916 season with a record of sixteen wins and ten losses. Earl also played center field and batted .350 with a .441 on-base percentage.[8] Essentially, Earl had done for the Royal Giants in 1916 what Lloyd had done for the Stars the year before. He provided on- and off-the-field leadership, and he was able to get his players to be a better team.

Royal Giants—Ridge Grounds—Brooklyn, New York (1916). Sykes stands in the back row, center.

Frank Sykes's first appearance for the Brooklyn Royal Giants came as a reliever in the Stars' nine-to-seven win against the Camden Athletic Club.[9] As a starter, he was never able to settle into a steady rhythm. He lost his first decision, four to three, to the Long Branch Cubans.[10] He would win his next two starts, but in a rematch against Long Branch, he pitched poorly. The four-to-three score was identical to the earlier game, but the Cubans dominated. Sykes allowed eighteen hits and walked three, with four strikeouts.[11] In his next start, the St. Louis Giants "hammered" him "for eight hits and six runs in three" innings.[12] Even his victories were not impressive. He allowed eight runs as the Stars managed to score ten in one of his last games for the team.[13] In September, a news report indicated that the Stars were "minus the services of . . . Sykes, who has left for school."[14] The news story was correct on both counts, but in truth, he had started to play for the Brooklyn Royal Giants.

On September 1, *The Standard Union* announced that "Sykes, the crack twirler . . . left this morning for Sharon, Conn. to join the Brooklyn Royal Giants."[15] His old teammate, Louis Santop, went with him. Sykes would join a staff that included Lefty Harvey, String Bean Williams, and Red Smith. In "Schoolboy" Sykes's first start, he "gave a fine exhibition of pitching." The Royal Giants won six to one.[16] Balancing his classwork and his on-field play, Sykes was a different pitcher for the Royal Giants than he had been for the Stars. He would win three more games in September and lose just one. He allowed, over his three wins, just four total runs, pitching a shutout against the Norfolk Reds on four hits.[17] His only loss came against his old team, the Lincoln Giants. He gave up eight runs and twelve hits. He hit a batter, walked a batter, and threw a wild pitch. In that start, Sykes "deserved a closer score than what was the result."[18] With the Royal Giants, Frank Sykes lived up to his billing as a "crack twiller." He established himself as an elite pitcher with Brooklyn, attracting the attention of Ed Bolden, owner of the Hilldale team, who recruited Sykes for the 1917 season.

1917: The Hilldale Baseball and Exhibition Company

Hilldale's story began in 1910 when Austin Devere Thompson, a nineteen-year-old man who enjoyed playing ball, organized the

Hilldale Athletic Club so African American boys and girls could learn how to play baseball. "Ranging from ages 14 to 17, most of the players were young workmen from Darby and nearby communities."[19] The team grew and, in 1911, attracted the attention of Ed Bolden, who worked as a clerk in Philadelphia's Central Post Office. "Playing on a vacant lot on Tenth Street, Darby were a crowd of young colored boys playing ball during the summer months. They seemed happy and drew quite a few spectators at some of their games. . . . One Saturday in June, there was a heated contest played between these colored lads and some colored boys from Philadelphia. Edward Bolden . . . was an eyewitness at this game and was asked to umpire." Bolden declined but agreed to keep score. After the Darby team won the game, Ed Bolden offered to buy them new hats. The delighted young men "asked him as a special favor to manage the team." He agreed.[20] "Quiet yet ambitious, Bolden immediately began to make changes."[21] Under his guidance, Hilldale grew from a loose association of young men who enjoyed playing ball into a team that would win three consecutive Eastern Colored League pennants and, in 1925, the Negro League World Series. In 1923, Bolden became chairman of the Eastern Colored League.[22]

The formation of those championship teams began in 1916, when Ed Bolden formally developed a five-year plan for his club. He "held nearly weekly meetings with his players at his home in Darby and made plans for substantial changes in the team's operation. The grounds were improved, new blue-gray uniforms were ordered, and a new grandstand was built."[23] Specifically, he modernized and expanded Hilldale Park. He more actively marketed his team, arranging for their uniforms to go on "display in the window of Marshall E. Smith on Eighth Street below Market" in Philadelphia.[24] "More significantly, Bolden implemented a stern new set of rules. . . . Absence from games, except for unavoidable reasons, was punishable by a $5 fine unless a three-day notice was given. Players were expected to attend practices twice a week in addition to a 30-minute practice before games."[25] In January 1917, he received the official certificate for a new corporation named "The Hilldale Baseball and Exhibition Company." He then set out to recruit a team and signed Frank Sykes, who would join the club after his spring semester ended.[26] In a testament to his developing reputation, not just among baseball managers and executives but also among casual fans, newspapers across the country covered the signing. The *Philadelphia Tribune* ran the headline "Hilldale lands pitcher Sykes," telling its readers that the club "was fortunate in signing" him.[27] The *Chicago Defender* declared that "he will make a good addition to the team."[28] *The New York Age*'s coverage was more staid, perhaps because their readers might have had hopes for him returning to Brooklyn. Their story stated that "Manager Bolden of the Hilldale Baseball Club has signed Sykes, formerly of the Brooklyn Giants, for the season."[29] He immediately "stabilized the team's previously shaky pitching."[30] In one of Frank Sykes's first appearances at Hilldale Park that season, he played against Hilldale for Howard University in an exhibition game. However, he did not pitch against his new team—he played center field.[31] Ed Bolden was protecting his investment. Hilldale defeated Howard, one to zero.

Hilldale Baseball Club (1916)

Sykes's record while pitching for Hilldale was thirteen wins and five losses.[32] Five of his wins would be on shutouts, and he pitched another ten innings in relief without allowing a run. The news accounts are uniform in their praise. In his first start for Hilldale, the *Philadelphia Tribune* tells its readers that "Sykes was an enigma to the [Norristown] Giants," demonstrating "masterful pitching."[33] When he shut out Logan Square in his next start, the papers wrote that "no one had been able to cross the home plate in the face of his air-tight pitching."[34] He would face Logan Square again in late July, allowing one run on five hits. In that game, "Sykes toyed with the heavy hitters."[35] In a game against J. G. Brill, "Sykes had the heavy hitters . . . at his mercy."[36] Against Wildwood, his pitches were "a puzzle."[37] In one of his final starts of the season, he pitched Hilldale to a fourteen-to-zero victory over Norwood. They "couldn't fathom" his pitching.[38] Even in his few losses, he impressed. In a three-to-zero loss to the Bacharach Giants, "Sykes pulled through several tight holes and pitched good ball except in the sixth inning, when he wobbled and allowed a couple of hits."[39] Against the Cuban Stars, another professional Black team, Sykes lost, but he "pitched well." He demonstrated his ability to "master the situation."[40]

His most impressive game of the season came against his old team, the Brooklyn Royal Giants. Sykes led Hilldale to a nine-to-one win. The *Philadelphia Tribune* proclaimed that "too much Sykes killed the Royals." Indeed, he did—Brooklyn had one run on five hits. Moreover, as a batter, Sykes had four hits, including a triple.[41] The *Chicago Defender* hailed his "brilliant pitching" and told their readers that he held "the hard hitting Giants in the hollow of his hand."[42] In looking back on his season, the *Philadelphia Tribune* noted that he had shown "the class of ball" he was "capable of throwing."[43] It was Frank Sykes's first full season with the same team, and it would be the last season he would have to balance his studies at Howard University's dental college with his baseball career. In the spring of 1918, he would graduate with his doctorate. He would be able to choose between a baseball career or a dental practice. Ultimately, he would choose to pursue both. The following season, he would be just twenty-six years old; he was in his prime. Nothing could hold him back—nothing, that is, that was under his control. The United States would enter the First World War. The European conflict had engulfed the United States, and the lives of many young men and women would be altered.

1918–1919

When Frank Sykes filled out his draft registration in 1917, he wrote on his forms that he "would like one more year in which to complete" his "studies in dentistry."[44] He would have that year and a few months more before he reported to the military for service. Sykes, as detailed in the *Philadelphia Tribune*, "left after Saturday's game [June 29] to visit his parents in Decatur, Alabama, before being called to colors," a colloquialism for being drafted into service.[45] He had been enlisted in the army on December 18, 1917. He was able to complete his degree and pitch for Hilldale for the first half of the season. The nature of Sykes's service is not clear beyond being discharged on April 21, 1919.[46] The Armistice, ending the war, came on November 11, 1918, so it is not likely he was stationed overseas. What is certain is that after June 1918, he would not pitch again for Hilldale and would not play more than a few games in organized ball until the 1920 season.

As the 1918 season began, however, he had cause for considerable optimism—he was named the team's captain and opening-day starter in April.[47] Through the end of June, he would compile a record of six wins and one loss.[48] He was truly impressive in those games. On opening day, he pitched Hilldale to a twelve-to-one victory over the Royal Giants. In May, he spoiled the Bacharachs Giants' home opener with his "wonderful hurling."[49] He "displayed perfect control, lots of pep, and pitched air-tight ball." The only run came on a passed ball.[50] In a June start against the Bacharachs, he struck out seven in a nineteen-to-three win. At the plate, he had two hits and scored two runs.[51] His final game for Hilldale came on June 26, just three days before he left the team. He helped them defeat the St. Louis Americans six to one, and "pitched fine ball."[52]

Service to his country put his career on hold for the remainder of the 1918 season and for the whole of 1919. In August, the *Philadelphia Tribune* reported that Frank Sykes, "formerly of the Hilldale team, was the official score-keeper" for a Philadelphia Giants doubleheader.[53] A year later, he pitched in relief for the Pennsylvania Rail Road Red Caps in their nine-to-seven loss to the Bacharach Giants. He appears in one other box score in 1919, playing right field for the Red Caps. He had two hits, including a triple, in a loss.[54] He also played for the Norfolk All-Stars, but no box scores survive to reveal the number or any details of his work.[55]

Sykes's sporadic service suggests that he was managing to stay in the game on a limited basis while he fulfilled his military commitment. After he completed his service requirements, he would pitch in relief and play in the field, suggesting he may not have been in ideal physical condition to play ball, let alone be the star pitcher he had been. His career as a pitcher would resume in 1920 when he would move to Baltimore and settle into that city's

African American community and anchor the Black Sox staff.

Frank Sykes's career as a baseball player was affected by the First World War, racism, and segregation. He and his teammates, the African American community, and the nation would confront those same issues. He performed well on the baseball field—well enough to have played in the major leagues, if custom allowed. He also served his country. The same cannot be said of other ballplayers. On June 1, 1916, the same day *The New York Age* reported that Frank Sykes had arrived in the city and reported on issues of racism and segregation in military service, the *New York Times* covered the game between the Chicago White Sox and the Detroit Tigers under the headline, "Jackson on Rampage." He hit two doubles, a triple, and a single in four at bats.[56] Unlike Frank Sykes, Shoeless Joe Jackson would avoid service in 1918 by acquiring a deferment to work an "essential job" at the Harlan and Hollingsworth Shipyards in Wilmington, Delaware. Although Jackson's major-league career was interrupted, he continued to play baseball. He was a star for Harlan's team in the Shipyard League. The story of Jackson's time with Harlan and Hollingsworth highlights stories of war, service, and racial privilege. The same month Jackson joined the shipyard team, Lewis Taylor, an African American who had worked at Harlan and Hollingsworth as a machinist, was mortally wounded in the Champagne-Marne offensive. Lewis served with the Ninety-Third Division and the 369th Infantry ("The Harlem Hellfighters"). He was shipped back to the Bronx Lebanon Hospital in New York, where he died on October 9. Less than two miles away, Harlan had played a game in the Shipyard Championship series at the Polo Grounds that September. After the Armistice,

Shoeless Joe Jackson and the other major leaguers who played for the shipyard teams returned to their major league teams for the 1919 season. Jackson was, ultimately, banned from baseball for his part in the scandal surrounding the 1919 World Series. Lewis Taylor's family was able to afford a headstone to mark his grave in 1928, ten years after his death. The headstone in Mount Olive Cemetery stands just three miles from the former site of Harlan Park, where Jackson played baseball the summer Lewis Taylor fought and died for his country.[57]

CHAPTER 7

TEASING THE ATMOSPHERE

DOC SYKES IN BALTIMORE, 1920-1926

Frank Sykes had served his country, received his doctorate in dentistry, and pitched in professional baseball. He was twenty-eight years old—the future must have seemed full of promise. The economy was poised for a post-war boom. Nonetheless, racism endured. Segregation remained the practice—if not the law—nationwide. Lynching persisted. Frank Sykes had seen the plight of African Americans in the South, North, and Midwest. He was born in Alabama, seasoned by traveling throughout the nation as a ballplayer, and educated at Atlantic Baptist College (Morehouse College) and Howard University. He was about to start his professional career. He had an opportunity to establish himself in a new community and with a new team; he could live anywhere.

He chose Baltimore, Maryland. He settled into an apartment at 1314 Pennsylvania Avenue and started work as a dentist. His neighbors, with the exception of a Russian-immigrant family of three, were African Americans. Most of them had also immigrated to Baltimore from various locations in the South: Virginia, Tennessee, North Carolina, and South Carolina. One neighbor, Lily James, was also from Alabama. She worked as a hairdresser and lived with her husband, Edward, who worked as a porter. It's tempting to think Frank Sykes would have met Lily and Edward and shared stories about their home state. Indeed, the neighborhood must have reminded Frank Sykes of his community in Decatur. Like Old Town, his neighbors on Pennsylvania Avenue could read and write, with the exception of the immigrant family from Russia. Like the Old Town community, the families on Pennsylvania Avenue were from the middle class. They were cooks, factory workers, railroad employees, stevedores, porters, and hairdressers. He had found a home.[1]

His neighborhood was also part of a thriving African American community in the Druid Hill section of the city. Department stores, markets, furniture stores, and dry goods sat side by side with lawyers, doctors, pharmacists, and dentists. *The Afro* also had their offices on Druid Hill Avenue. Smith's Hotel, run by brothers Thomas and Wallace, sat across the street from *The Afro*. Thomas took charge of the financial aspects of the business and was active in Democratic Party politics. Wallace handled advertisement and marketing. The brothers had started several successful businesses in the city before buying the hotel. Wallace owned a coal delivery service, and Tom ran a saloon. Like Frank Sykes's father, Wallace had been born into slavery. The brothers' hotel was a more-or-less permanent home to several Black Sox players and a home away from home for players from visiting Black professional teams. It is likely that Frank Sykes stayed there while playing for Hilldale and the Royal Giants. At the hotel's bar, reporters, athletes, local businessmen, and professionals mingled. It was the social center of the Druid Hill community.

About a half mile away from *The Afro*'s office and Smith's Hotel, Howard Young ran a pharmacy. Frank Sykes's apartment was just around the corner. Young's pharmacy was the first in Baltimore to be owned by an African American. Like Sykes, Young was a graduate of Howard University. He was also active in the Civil Rights Movement. When the railroads proposed separate cars for African Americans, Young spoke in opposition: "We should make a vigorous protest against it. Once the thing starts we will see no end to segregation in Maryland, and our people will be the only sufferers."[2] In protest of segregated housing, Young purchased a home in a white neighborhood, challenging the law.[3] The front page of *The Afro* read, "Dr. Young Expects All to Help."[4]

Howard Young was also an influential member of the NAACP. His success and activism highlight what life was like for young African American professionals living in Baltimore in the first decades of the twentieth century. The city did offer economic opportunities for men like Sykes and Young. There was a closely knit African American community, but Baltimore was a city deeply divided along racial lines, with many Eastern European immigrant communities sometimes aligned with and sometimes opposed to the African American community's interests. For example, in the early twentieth century, literacy tests written in English threatened to take voting rights away from African Americans and those citizens for whom English was a second language.[5]

Blacks and non-English-speaking immigrants united in opposition to the law. A decade later, Baltimore's mayor and city council passed and enforced a series of laws prohibiting Black families from moving into white neighborhoods.[6] These laws became a model for segregation laws throughout the country and resulted in the confinement of a growing Black population into increasingly congested sections of the city. The immigrant community was not openly opposed to the segregation laws. Baltimore in general and the Druid Hill Avenue neighborhood offered both opportunities and hostilities for Dr. Sykes. Understandably, resuming his baseball career may not have been under consideration.

However, in the early spring, he began to seriously think about getting back into the game. Initially, he thought he might move into the business end of baseball rather than as a player. In March, he entered into serious discussions with Dr. J. H. Hayes and John Hayes, "a well known Druid Hill Avenue merchant," about forming a new team. They looked at purchasing land to build a new ballpark, and they had chosen a name, "Fighting Buffaloes," to honor "colored fighters who lie buried in the war-swept soil in France."[7] It was an intriguing idea, and perhaps catalyzed by a desire for African Americans to own an African American professional team. Charles Spedden, a white man, owned the Baltimore Black Sox, and although he had a good reputation in the African American community, there was recurring talk about African Americans becoming more involved in the business of Black baseball in Baltimore. The "Fighting Buffaloes" never took the field, and there is no evidence the proposal endured beyond a nascent stage.

Doc Sykes and the Baltimore Black Sox

Frank "Doc" Sykes would sign with the Baltimore Black Sox. The Black Sox could trace their origins to a team called the Weldons, founded in 1905 by Wallace Smith. The Weldons would change names, becoming variously the Weldon Giants and the Baltimore Giants. Ownership would change hands, and when a group of white businessmen took over the team in 1912, the players left. Those same players would reemerge in 1913 as the Baltimore Black Sox. Howard Young was the team's president, and the Smith family were strong financial backers. The Black Sox made various fields around the city their home grounds and found some success, but by 1917, they were in danger of folding.

Charles Spedden stepped in. He worked in the Coal and Coke division of the Baltimore and Ohio Railroad. He purchased the team and moved them into the home grounds of the B&O Railroad's industrial-league club. After a year, that ballpark, the Westport Baseball Grounds, became known as Black Sox Park. In 1920, Spedden began construction of a new ballpark, wholly owned and financed by the club. Maryland Park, too, would become known as Black Sox Park. Spedden had done for the Black Sox what Ed Bolden had done for Hilldale—they had become teams of professionals.

The clubs would also become rivals in the Eastern Colored League. In 1920, Spedden had scouted for talent to add to the Black Sox roster. The team needed at least one more strong hitter and one more strong pitcher. Jud Wilson proved to be the hitter. He played for the Black Sox for ten years before moving to Hilldale. Wilson was elected to baseball's Hall of Fame in 2006. He owns the fourth highest career batting average (.350) in major league history, behind only Ty Cobb (.366), Rogers Hornsby (.358), and Shoeless Joe Jackson (.356). To strengthen the Black Sox staff, Spedden recruited Doc Sykes.

Sykes would pitch for the Black Sox for five seasons. His most impressive games came in 1922, with a no-hitter against the Bacharach Giants and a win against a team of major-league all-stars. In 1920, available records indicate that he won four games while losing three.[8] He pitched in several other games, but no box scores or results survived. He was the scheduled pitcher in June against the Norfolk All-Stars, one of the teams Sykes pitched for in 1919.[9] He also played center field in a few games.[10] His most impressive work came late in the season against three teams: the Bacharach Giants, Hilldale, and the Roanoke Giants. In early September, he "narrowly miss[ed] getting a no-hit game" against Roanoke. He carried a no-hitter into the ninth, and with two outs, the Black Sox committed three consecutive errors. A bunt hit scored the winning run. Sykes did strike out nine Giants.[11] In a series of September games played at Harlan Field in Wilmington, Delaware, against Sykes's old team, Hilldale, he would win one game and lose the second. He pitched well in both. The first game was heralded as "the largest attraction in local baseball." Wilmington would host numerous games between African American professional teams in the 1920s. Sykes won the game four to three, allowing three runs on seven hits while striking out five and walking two. He held his old teammate, Louis Santop, hitless. Sykes lost the second game of the series, one to zero. Both "pitchers battled," but the Black Sox only managed one hit. Santop got the better of his old friend, managing just one hit but scoring the game's only run.[12] In the season's final game against the Bacharachs, Sykes lost five to zero. He had completed his first full year of professional baseball.

In 1921, the Black Sox and Frank Sykes reached an agreement well before the season started. In February, *The Afro* made the announcement that he would be on the team.[13] He was also their opening day starting pitcher—although, apparently by design, he pitched just two innings and then moved to center field. As a pitcher, he struck out two batters, allowing no runs. As a batter, he had a hit and a sacrifice. The Black Sox won the game seven to one, using three pitchers and rotating them through the field before or after their appearances.[14]

Sykes's first recorded victory of the season came against the Rexmen, a local semipro team. He pitched a complete game in the Black Sox five-to-three win, allowing no walks but earning six strikeouts. He also hit a batter.[15] His record that season was fifteen wins against two losses. He pitched poorly in only one game, a seven-to-six loss to the American Chain Company, a local semipro team.[16]

He threw two shutouts in consecutive starts in June against the Parksides and the American Chain Company.[17] His most impressive wins came in September against two African American professional teams, the Harrisburg Giants and Hilldale. Against Harrisburg, Sykes allowed a walk and two runs and struck out ten in a ten-to-two win. The Black Sox played Hilldale at Harlan Field in Wilmington. They were a last-minute replacement; Hilldale was scheduled to play the Bacharachs, who could not make it to Wilmington on time. Even without being able to prepare for the game, he pitched the Black Sox to a six-to-one victory, allowing just five hits and walking a batter while striking out six. His performance impressed: "Sykes stopped the Hilldale crew more completely than any other pitcher who has opposed Bolden's crew this season."[18] It was a dramatic moment—Bolden watched the man he had signed to a contract years before dominate his team. Indeed, an "intense rivalry . . . exist[ed] between the clubs." When Baltimore played Hilldale, it was inevitably a "bitter battle." During a July game, which the Black Sox and Sykes would win, there was a "near riot." Joe Lewis, the Black Sox catcher, attacked an umpire over an inconsistent strike zone.[19] Victories over Hilldale must have been satisfying to Doc Sykes, but he was far more likely to have a sense of nostalgia than vengeance; Bolden had treated him well. Sykes had pleasant memories of Hilldale, and if not for the war, he may have stayed with them. He had also settled in Baltimore, often volunteering in the local community. He umpired the regional high school baseball championship game.[20] His dental practice was thriving. Reporting on his pitching, the news reports would often reference his profession, in one instance calling him a "rangy tooth extractor."[21] He was also a part of a vibrant and growing African American community. He was the star pitcher for the Black Sox, and in mid-season, he was named as an officer in the newly incorporated "Black Sox Baseball and Exhibition Club."[22]

He was also named the Black Sox's "best pitcher"[23] in 1922. He would win crucial games not only against Hilldale but also against a team of major-league stars. He pitched a no-hitter against the Bacharach Giants, one of his four shutouts that season. In ten additional games, he allowed two runs or less. Even more impressive, he was the winning pitcher in 30 percent of Black Sox games. With him, they won 85 percent of their games. Without him pitching, they were still an impressive team, winning 67 percent of the time. He was clearly their most valuable player, and the Black Sox were an exceptional team.[24] Randall Cassell, writing for the *Evening Sun*, noted that they "have made quite a reputation on the diamond. With the passing of each game played the colored professional ball team of Westport is being sought for games of the best pro teams in the East." Cassell was a white sports columnist, writing for the region's premier white newspaper. He championed the Black Sox and Doc Sykes, about whom he wrote that he "was going in fine style" that season. He called them a "professional" team, deserving of the respect of "pro teams," both white and African American. He also noted that the Black Sox "have proved an attraction in every town they have appeared in so far, and the fans troop out in large numbers to watch the Baltimoreans play." He, significantly, sees the team as a marker of pride for the entire city, regardless of race.[25]

The ability to draw from all the city's ethnic and racial groups was on display in a June game. Doc Sykes pitched before 18,000 fans at Oriole Park.[26] Maryland Park, also known as Black Sox Park, could only accommodate 12,000 to 14,000 spectators. The Black Sox were poised to become a premier franchise in the Eastern Colored League.

The Black Sox were gearing up for the inaugural season in the Eastern Colored League (ECL). The team put in new fences, a new grandstand, showers, and lockers. The field had been leveled and reseeded. The right-field fence was moved back by thirty-five feet. Charles Spedden, the team's owner, also brought in additional players, like catcher Julio Rojo, who had played for the Bacharachs and Cuban Stars. He was a good hitter, but he made his career on his reputation for calling how a game was pitched and for handling a pitching staff. The team also added new pitchers for the season in February to take the load off of Doc Sykes.[27] He would be thirty-two years old and had just completed his most successful year in baseball. In his first start in front of a sell-out crowd at Maryland Park (Black Sox Park), he shut out the Bacharach Giants, the team he had no-hit a few months before.[28] Sykes and the team seemed well positioned to have a great season.

However, something was wrong—he would pitch exceptionally well in one start and then be badly beaten in the next. He allowed twelve runs to the Brooklyn Royal Giants, and he then shut down Hilldale, allowing a run on four hits. In his next start, he lost to Hilldale, allowing eight runs, only to limit the Cuban Stars to a run in his next game.[29] After giving up ten runs to the Washington Potomacs and lasting less than two innings to the Bacharachs, the fans started to express concerns: "The fans were heard to wonder what was the matter with 'Doc.' Well, they should," wrote the reporter for *The Afro*. "After the game, 'Doc' was heard to remark . . . that he didn't know himself."[30] In August, he could not finish the second inning of a game. *The Afro* reported that "Sykes had been held back for this game [the second of a doubleheader] doubtless in the belief that old man jinx, who has been on his trail continuously, would think he wasn't going to work, and thus would go elsewhere. But jinx was right on the job as usual." Sykes was lifted in the second after walking three men, yielding two hits, and making a wild peg to first, all of which totaled four runs. A caricature accompanied the news story, showing Sykes being chased by a devil-like figure labeled "jinx."[31]

Doc Sykes's role with the Black Sox ended, temporarily, a week later. *The Afro* speculated that he had "been suspended because he has been unable to pitch winning baseball."[32] The Black Sox did not officially release him, but he subsequently started pitching in non-ECL games for Hilldale, with the *Pittsburgh Courier* telling its readers that "Doc Sykes has been loaned to manager Lloyd by the Baltimore Black Sox for ten days."[33] In September, Sykes published a letter in *The Afro* addressed to "my patients and friends," writing that "I am no longer connected with the Baltimore Black Sox baseball team. I am now giving my time to my dental practice." In November, the Black Sox officially released him.[34]

Early in 1924, Charles Spedden explained that Sykes had never been "suspended." Confirming the report in *The Courier*, Spedden explained that at "the end of last season, Manager Ed Bolden of the Hilldales was short of pitchers. . . . We loaned Sykes to Hilldale, and he won two out of three games he pitched, enabling Hilldale to win the Philadelphia Baseball Association championship."[35] Cynics might rightly doubt Spedden's performance of generosity to a rival club. In reality, the Black Sox likely made a deal with Bolden, allowing Sykes to pitch in non-league games, permitting Bolden to reserve his best pitcher for ECL opponents. In return, Sykes and the Black Sox would benefit in that he could try to work things out against lesser competition. Also, a change of scenery might just get rid of the "jinx."

Irrespective of Sykes's announced retirement and his official release, he resigned with the Black Sox for the 1924 season, again pitching unevenly. He did have his moments—in one of the final games of his professional career, he pitched a twelve-inning shutout against the Cubans, giving up only four hits. The *Philadelphia Tribune* covered the game, telling its readers that Sykes was a "former Hilldale luminary" and included a photo of him in a Hilldale uniform.[36] Although he would win at least one more game, he faltered in a series of starts. In August, *The Afro* announced his retirement. Officially, the Black Sox gave him his "unconditional release" because of his "inability to travel with the team." He was asked to turn in his uniform. He would devote his time to his dental practice. Tributes poured in. *The Afro* told its readers that he has been a "fixture on the Black Sox Club for a number of years." Norfolk's *New Journal and Guide* called him "one of the greatest Negro ball pitchers of the time."[37] Doc Sykes's playing career had ended.

His career as a dentist would continue, and in 1924, it appeared that he would settle into Baltimore's professional African American community for a long time. However, less than nine months after his retirement from baseball, he received news that his father, Solomon Sykes, had passed away. He made the decision to leave the city and the dental practice he had so diligently built and return to Decatur. *The Afro* reported that "Dr. Sykes does not expect to return to Baltimore for at least five years. He intends to manage the business affairs of his mother and attend to the education of a young sister."[38] His decision speaks to his values—he would sacrifice the life he had built in order to help his family. His actions are commendable, but we should acknowledge the price he would pay. He could have settled in the city and continued to build his medical practice. He could have raised his family in another city and in another community that loved him both because of his work as a dentist and also as a ballplayer. If not Baltimore, he could have settled in any of the places where he had played (Washington, Philadelphia, Norfolk, or New York). He would have been able to establish himself and his practice there and build on his reputation as a ballplayer to build his practice. He would give up those opportunities and return to support his family. It should also be noted that he would be leaving the urban centers of the Mid-Atlantic for the Deep South. As difficult as life was for African Americans in Baltimore, life in Alabama was even more challenging.

CHAPTER 8

QUIET AND MODEST

FRANK SYKES AS A FAMILY MAN

Asberry Murry died just after sunset on a chilly Sunday evening in October 1925. He was sixty-nine, and his once strong body was giving out. He did have a job—picking cotton on a nearby farm—but he could only work about two hours each day and had not been able to work for weeks. Seenie Murry, his wife, explained that her husband went out for a walk at about 5:30 p.m. He may have needed to visit the outhouse, as his body was found close by. He may have wanted to check on their small garden as there had been a light frost the night before. Or he may have just wanted a quiet draw on his pipe, which was found near where Ethel Turner and Rosa Phillips heard shots. They went out to investigate the noise, navigating as best they could through the twilight. A dog was barking nearby, and they recalled seeing what they believed was a light. When they reached the location where they thought the noise had originated, they looked around and found Murry's corncob pipe. They saw, in the near-darkness, what might have been blood. Rosa saw two white men nearby and decided to approach them. Ethel did not join her. As Rosa drew near, she saw Asberry Murry's body, stretched out and lying on his back. His arms had been folded across his chest, and his hat covered his face. She testified that she knew Asberry Murry well enough to know it was him, even with his face covered. He wore no shoes. They were too painful to cover his feet, swollen from decades of hard labor. Rosa confronted the men, who identified themselves as police officers, Monroe West and Robert Stewart. Officer West indicated that he had shot Murry in self-defense.[1]

West and Stewart were hunting bootleggers in the neighborhood and had separated to cover more ground. Officer Stewart testified that he heard West call his name and then heard gunshots. Stewart found West on the ground. A few feet away was the body of a man later identified as Asberry Murry. Stewart explained that Murry was dead, but his body remained hunched in a kneeling position. The officers moved the body and positioned it as Rosa Phillips described. The police notified Seenie but not before taking Asberry Murry to Sykes's undertakers. Frank's brother, Leo, answered the late call and carefully recorded the wounds. Seenie asked not to see her husband in that condition, so her son met with Leo Sykes. In court, they testified that Asberry Murry had been shot three times, with entry wounds in the back of the head, in the back of the neck, and in the back of the shoulder. On November 7, Seenie signed an affidavit, and Officers Stewart and West were arrested for first-degree murder. The trial attracted large crowds and enormous public interest. When the jury delivered its verdicts, Robert Stewart was acquitted on all charges, and Monroe West, who tried to claim Stewart had fired the shots that killed Murry, was convicted of involuntary manslaughter and sentenced to seven years in prison. He would never serve time.

He not only remained free while he appealed his conviction but continued to work as a police officer in Albany, where he would face additional charges for assault in an unrelated case. He was then hired to be chief of police in Falkville, Alabama. In May 1927, the state Court of Appeals upheld his conviction, and in October, the state supreme court refused to hear his case. He nonetheless remained free, pending the Board of Pardons' review. Two thousand five hundred people signed a petition asking the board to grant him parole. The newspapers, when not asking his views on the Falkville basketball or football team, told their readers that Asberry Murry was an "alleged bootlegger" who "attacked the officer with a bottle." West, in their view, acted in "self-defense."[2] The news stories failed to mention that West shot Murry in the back three times or that he was in such poor health, he could barely walk, let alone threaten anyone. The courts had taken those factors into account. The Board of Pardons did as well, voting two to one not to grant him parole on January 30, 1928. He was then scheduled to begin his seven-year sentence, but the governor intervened. Bibb Graves, a member of the Ku Klux Klan, paroled West the day after the Board of Pardons voted to send him to prison.

Frank Sykes moved from Baltimore to Decatur within six months of Asberry Murry's death and within a year of Solomon Sykes's passing. Frank was there, specifically, to help his mother and sister, but he would also contribute to the family businesses.

The "Sykes clan," as the papers noted in 1933, was comprised of three brothers and an uncle: "a physician [Newman], a dentist [Frank], and undertaker [Leo], and a businessman [Frank's uncle J. J.]."[3] Solomon Sykes had given his children an education and helped them establish their careers. He also passed onto them the reputation that he had "won for himself by his acts of kindness and many friends among both races."[4] He and his wife had also passed on to their sons a sense of moral obligation to stand up against injustice. Leo Sykes had testified at the trial of the white officer who murdered Asberry Murry. Frank would testify at the Scottsboro Boys trial a few years later, and the entire Sykes family would offer financial and moral support to the families devastated by the trial. The case of Murry and West offers a glimpse into the power dynamics of race, culture, and the law. The courts were starting to offer hope for African Americans, but law enforcement, elected officials, the media, and a large proportion of white Alabama residents not only opposed Civil Rights but openly discriminated against, beat, and killed African Americans. The Sykes family members were not the only ones fighting back. Increasingly, African Americans demanded equal rights, and the NAACP opened thirteen branches throughout Alabama in the 1920s, including an office in Decatur within a few weeks of Frank Sykes's arrival.[5]

The move to Decatur was not all turmoil. Doc Sykes was able to reestablish friendships and reacquaint himself with the places and the rhythms of life he had left behind to start his college and baseball careers. He could, once again, walk the streets of Old Town Decatur. He could see and hear the railroads, and the Tennessee

River and its traffic. He also, doubtlessly, valued the opportunities that living close to his mother, sisters, and brothers afforded. He had rejoined his family and returned to his hometown. He also started his own family. In July, he "motored to Philadelphia with his sisters and took home a charming bride in the former Miss Alice West."[6] Together, they would settle into their home at 405 Wills Street in Decatur.[7]

Alice West was born in Glen Mills, Pennsylvania, on April 13, 1903. She grew up with her two brothers in a working-class community in suburban Philadelphia. Her father, Julius, was from Virginia. Born in 1874, he migrated north for work and held a series of blue-collar jobs for the railroads. Alice's mother, Katie, was born in about 1880 in Durrow, in the Irish Midlands. Their marriage was a testament to their love for and commitment to one another. In many jurisdictions, marriage between an African American and a white person was illegal. In most places, the couple and their children would have been met with intolerance. Alice's family valued faith; she was raised a Catholic. They also valued education. Alice graduated from Temple University in 1924 with a degree in education. She started work in the Baltimore City public schools and took up residence at 1700 McCulloh Street in the Druid Hill section of the city. She lived just a few blocks from Frank Sykes's residence and his office. How they met remains a mystery, but they likely had met by Christmas 1924. Their names appear together on a list of those who had donated one dollar to fund Christmas dinners for orphans.[8]

Frank and Alice settled into life in Decatur. With the exception of the Scottsboro case, their lives could be those of any upper-middle-class family in the 1920s and 1930s. They did not seek publicity. His accomplishments and courage made him well known, but he was naturally "quiet and modest, almost to the point of reticence."[9] While in Decatur, they had three sons: Frank, born in 1929; Lawrence, born in 1931; and Charles, born in 1934. Dr. Sykes would attend professional functions in addition to serving his patients. As a "prominent dentist," he had been invited to attend the fiftieth anniversary of Tuskegee's founding, and he served as a regional vice president of the National Dental Association.[10] Frank Sykes and his wife would travel locally, notably attending the African American tenor Roland Hayes concert in Birmingham.[11] By the mid-to-late 1930s, Frank and Alice decided to leave Decatur and return to Baltimore. Their obligation to Frank's younger sisters had been fulfilled. His mother was getting older, but she was in good hands with a large family to support her. Moreover, the KKK had not stopped its campaign of harassment that began just after his testimony. Baltimore, a city with its own issues of race and prejudice, was nonetheless a safer place to raise a family. In January 1938, they had returned to the city where Frank had first established himself as a dentist and played ball, and where Alice had worked as a teacher.

The Afro explained to its readers that "Dr. Sykes" now "makes his home in Baltimore." He "had built up a good dental practice in Decatur" but "decided" to reestablish himself as a dentist in the city, opening "a dental office on the corner of Monument and Caroline Streets."[12] Baltimore was beginning to emerge from the Depression, so the financial prospects for renewing his practice were better than they had been since 1929. In the early decades of the twentieth century, Baltimore had established itself as a center for trade, manufacturing, and food processing. The grain and coal that passed through the city, as well as the food that was canned there, meant that Baltimore was a major trading center for both railroads and ship traffic. Consequently, the Great Depression was slow in coming to the city, but by 1932, it was beginning to take effect, and although Baltimore's "situation was not so dire as that in other parts of the country," jobs in manufacturing and in the unskilled labor force had disappeared at an alarming rate.[13] Because of discriminatory policies in education and housing, those economic losses hit the African American community particularly hard. It would not have been advisable for Frank Sykes to move his family according to his original timeline of about five years.

The city's economy and the demand for unskilled labor began to rise in the mid-to-late 1930s. With Japan's increasing hostilities in China, Italian incursions into East Africa, and the Spanish Civil War, demand for coal, steel, and grain increased. Baltimore found itself in a precarious but lucrative position. On August 21, 1937, in Port Covington, a British steamer loaded supplies bound for China while a Dutch steamer simultaneously loaded steel bound for Japan. Prior to US involvement in World War II, ships would dock in Baltimore, oftentimes hull to hull, bearing the flags of the Soviet Union, Japan, Italy, Great Britain, and Nazi Germany. With the growing hostilities between warring nations, all port activity was fraught with danger. In October 1940, the British freighter *Waziristan* trained her guns on the Italian-flagged ship *Euro*, loaded with scrap iron. The Italian captain decided to "abandon the trip."[14] The war trade was also lucrative. At the Western Maryland Railyards in Port Covington and the Baltimore and Ohio yards in Locust Point, there were plans for steel mills and new warehouses. Rail tracks were repaired and expanded "for the first time in years."[15] Despite the tension and danger, the economy was strong enough to support new businesses or the reestablishment of a dental practice.

Race relations in the city and the nation were also improving, although horrifying instances of racism and bigotry persisted. The issue of *The Afro* from January 8, 1938, which featured the story of Frank Sykes's return and an accompanying photo from the Scottsboro Boys trials, offers a glimpse into the issues the African American community faced. A feature story discussed W. E. B. Du Bois's change in emphasis from the "top ten percent" of African Americans to a "new economic order" and a "new attitude towards labor." He stressed that the community must have "work and income" to enjoy "life, liberty, and happiness."[16] The organization he founded was, indeed, making progress. Other stories in *The Afro* from that day explain how the NAACP pressed the Pennsylvania Railroad in Baltimore to issue a statement that it "will not tolerate any discriminatory treatment of colored passengers on the part of Yellow cab drivers," and that the Railroad will "punish Jim Crow cabbies" that practice racism.[17] The story directly above the photo of Dr. Sykes carried the headline that "Calvert County Grants Equal Teacher Salaries," indicating that the fight for equal pay for African American teachers is "one of the fruits of the legal fight by Thurgood Marshall and other NAACP attorneys in Maryland."[18] Other stories in that issue of *The Afro* confront the racism that permeated American society, noting that there were eight lynchings in 1937 with no arrests and that a white café owner would not serve African Americans.[19]

Other news focused on cultural issues. Columnist Lillian Johnson lamented that there was "not a single, colored drama on Broadway or on tour," expressing hope that the theater would "give the colored man a chance to come before the public in a role a little better than the ignorant, fighting alley people that have been portrayed in some of the productions of the past."[20] Conversely, the front-page story in that week's *The Afro* hailed a film titled *Spirit of Youth,* which featured Joe Louis in a semi-autobiographical role. He played a boxer named Joe Thomas. George Murphy, *The Afro*'s editor, noted that the film contained "no epithets, nothing of the clown-like performances that have generally characterized all-colored cast pictures." Instead, it was a "good, clean, simple . . . story in which the poor boy, by hard struggle wins the pot of gold and the girl."[21] In presenting the news from the first week of 1938 to its readers, *The Afro* gave a clear picture of the challenges and horrors the African American community faced, but it also showed the progress possible through agitation and concerted, community-based action. In this context, the editors of *The Afro* could have chosen any photo of Doc Sykes to accompany the story of his return to Baltimore. They did not choose a photo of him in his Black Sox uniform or any of the other photos on file—instead, they chose to use the photo taken of him during his testimony in the Morgan County Courthouse in which he, with dignity and confidence, testified on behalf of the Scottsboro defendants. In making such a choice, they emphasized Frank Sykes, the man who had the courage to fight against racism and oppression.

Frank Sykes, with his wife, Alice, and his three boys settled into life in the city, buying a home at 1517 East Monument Street.[22] The family would grow. A daughter, Alice, was born in 1946, and they would move both home and office to 1209 East Preston Street.[23] His playing days were over, and as the Scottsboro case faded into history, Frank Sykes settled into the rhythms of raising a family and tending to his patients. He did testify in court again. He was "held up by 6 thugs" leaving his dental office one evening. He served as a witness for the prosecution.[24] He also served as vice chair for the Maryland Dental Society.[25] He was a leader in his field. He continued his commitment to Civil Rights, publicly backing opposition to the "Ober Bill," a proposed law under consideration in the Maryland state legislature that would have limited civil liberties.[26] He would also pitch for a final time, taking the mound at Memorial Stadium for an "Old Timers Game" in 1951.[27]

November 10, 1986, was a beautiful fall day in Baltimore, with partly cloudy skies and temperatures in the midfifties.[28] The lead stories in that morning's news included the return home of David Jacobsen, the director of the American University in Beirut's Medical Hospital, who was released after 532 days as a hostage. Corazon Aquino, the president of the Philippines, threatened to use "people power" to thwart a rumored military coup. In Beijing, the Chinese government sought to work with the United States to upgrade its military.[29] In baseball news, Cal Ripken Jr. led a team of American League all-stars to a nine-to-four win against a team of Japanese all-stars.[30] Locally, a federal judge "overturned the verdict of a jury that had found Tandy Corp. guilty of discriminating against metropolitan Baltimore blacks." The company had "excluded blacks from managing stores in white, more affluent areas."[31] These battles were no longer Dr. Frank Sykes's battles—the "pitcher and fighter against bigotry" passed away. Like his father thirty-one years before, he died of "complications from pulmonary pneumonia."[32] His legacy would survive him—in his family, in his fights for Civil Rights, and in baseball.

CHAPTER 9

PITCHER, DENTIST, HERO

Bill Glauber, writing for the *Baltimore Sun*, summed up Frank Sykes's life in three words: "pitcher, dentist, hero."[1] Glauber's focus was on the public man, but he might well have added father, brother, husband, friend, and son to reflect the totality of Frank Sykes's life and legacy. Indeed, a speaker at his memorial service likened his life to a traditional African American patchwork quilt. He brought to both his public and private lives all the squares of that quilt with a sense of devotion and integrity.

Doc Sykes's legacy as a ballplayer is largely unknown. He reached his zenith as a pitcher a year before the establishment of the Eastern Colored League. Consequently, his official major-league record lists seven wins against nine losses. He does have a positive WAR (wins above replacement) for his career (.5), but the record is necessarily flawed because it excludes his work for teams that would be part of the ECL and were as strong as other major league clubs of the period.[2] He would play alongside men who are now in the Hall of Fame in Cooperstown, notably Pete Hill and Jud Wilson. He would pitch against other Hall of Fame members, such as Judy Johnson and Oscar Charleston. However, Doc Sykes will never be inducted into Cooperstown because his best years as a pitcher came before the official establishment of the Negro Leagues. He stands beside many ballplayers whose race and the bigotries of American society prevented them from having an opportunity to play in the major leagues. He also lost a year and a half of his prime to military service. However, his contemporaries and baseball historians did and continue to recognize his value and his contributions to baseball in the first decades of the twentieth century. James Bready, writing in the *Baltimore Sun*, mentions Sykes as one of the premier players in Baltimore's baseball history.[3] In 1995, Salisbury State University featured Doc Sykes in an exhibit titled "Before You Can Say Jackie Robinson: Black Baseball in Maryland in the Era of the Colored Line, 1885-1950."[4] Sam Lacy in *The Afro* lists about a dozen Negro League greats. He mentions Sykes alongside Oscar Charleston, Martín Dihigo, Cool Papa Bell, Turkey Stearnes, and Bill Mackey. Lacy explains that his audience, white journalists, "listened with an obvious air of tolerance" as he "ran down a list of great colored players they and their world never got the opportunity to see."[5] Lacy offers an interesting perspective, emphasizing the loss to "their world." African American baseball fans saw men like Doc Sykes pitch. They knew his greatness—the loss is not theirs. The loss belongs to the society that could not see him play.

Frank Sykes's moral leadership and his work ethic animated his life as a ballplayer, and it's difficult to distinguish the pitcher from the Civil Rights pioneer, but Peter Dreier and Robert Elias articulate the two paths well in *Baseball Rebels*. They point out that "baseball rebels often make a mark on their sport speaking out against injustice while others remain silent. . . . Some ballplayers take even greater risks beyond the game." Dreier and Elias go on to write that Frank Sykes "knew what was at stake in the Scottsboro trials for himself and all African Americans, and with a growing national and international audience watching, he stepped up to help reform American criminal justice amidst a seriously hostile environment."[6] He paid a personal price for his courage. The Ku Klux Klan burned crosses at his home and his office in the immediate aftermath of the trial, and the violence persisted for years. Ultimately, he "was so harassed by Decatur's white citizens he felt the need to leave the city and spent the rest of his life in Baltimore."[7]

The environment in Baltimore was better, but he also faced bigotry there. When he first arrived in the city to play for the Black Sox, he was invited to join the Baltimore Dental Society, only to be rejected when "they learned that he was black."[8] The personal price he and his family paid was high. Nonetheless, by speaking out, he left a legacy that resonates through the history of American law. His articulate testimony and his willingness to make himself the target of hatred and violence led to the US Supreme Court's decision in *Norris v. Alabama* (1935), which ruled that racial bias in the selection of juries violated both the Sixth and Fourteenth Amendments. Every day, in courtrooms across the United States, defendants benefit from his sacrifices.

Lawrence Sykes, Frank's son, wrote about his father's legacy on his return to Decatur in 1979. Lawrence, in an attempt to get his bearings, looked around Decatur after a long absence. He wrote that he had to "scan and search for clues." He drove "past the Morgan County Courthouse" and imagined the "chamber haunted by the ghosts of the Scottsboro Boys and the testimony of 'Doc' Sykes," his father.[9] Larry Sykes embraced his father's legacy as his birthright. He was born in Decatur in 1931, the year of the first of the Scottsboro trials. He was educated at Dunbar High School in Baltimore, where he discovered his love for photography, earning money by taking "souvenir shots of the athletes."[10] After graduation, he continued his studies and played basketball for Morgan State and Long Island University. He also developed his craft as an artist, using photography but also "incorporating painting and drawing into composite pieces of art he called conjurgraphs."[11] He went on to teach in Ghana and at Rhode Island College and traveled widely, drawing inspiration for his work and life from those he met and the communities he encountered. He had a particular passion for the cultures of the African diaspora.[12] He passed away in 2020. Lawrence's older brother, Frank, was also born in Decatur in 1929, and was educated at Dunbar High School. He went on to study at UCLA and settled in Oakland.[13]

Morehouse College ceremony honoring Doc Sykes as the oldest living graduate (1982). The president of Morehouse College, Hugh Gloster, is to Doc Sykes's left.

Doc Sykes's surviving children include his daughter, Alice, and a son, Charles. Alice, the youngest child, was born in Baltimore in 1947. She received her MA from Howard University and worked for the University of the District of Columbia and for the United Negro College Fund. She is the family archivist and historian. Charles, like his brothers, was born in Decatur and educated at Dunbar High School in Baltimore. He went on to study at the Tilton School and at Middlebury College in Vermont, where he received his BA in political science (1957). While at Middlebury, Charles participated in its Reserve Officer Training Corps (ROTC) program and, after graduation, proceeded to serve two years as a commissioned officer in the United States Army, which included a thirteen-month assignment in Korea. He then went to work for

"Cooperative for Assistance and Relief Everywhere" (C.A.R.E.).[14] He was first stationed in Greece, but his work took him around the world. He helped communities in Poland—where he met his wife—Pakistan, India, Egypt, and the Dominican Republic. He was appointed by President Clinton to be an Assistant Deputy Secretary of State in 1994.[15]

Alice Sykes, Doc's wife, passed away in 1992 from pneumonia. Her funeral mass was held at St. Francis Xavier Roman Catholic Church in Baltimore. Her obituary remembers her as a teacher and fighter for Civil Rights. She successfully petitioned the Archbishop of Baltimore, Francis Keough, to integrate diocesan schools.[16]

Family photo on the occasion of Doc's ninetieth birthday celebration at Howard University, 1982. Seated (from right to left): Alice Sykes, Nana Swan, Eunice Stene, Amy Adam, Atenor Adam, Jr., Agnieszka Sykes. Standing (from right to left): Doc Sykes, Melvin Sykes, Reba Adam, Altenor Adam, Sr., Barbara Adam and Adrian Adam, Lawrence Sykes, Chris Sykes, Kirk Sykes, Lil Sykes, Barbara Sykes, Alice Sykes.

Frank Sykes's legacy extends from his family to the communities he touched in Baltimore. He organized health care professionals and devoted time to offering free and discounted health services to the city's poor. He also raised scholarship money for graduates of Baltimore City's schools to attend Howard University. At the conclusion of his memorial service, the pastor asked the gathering of friends and family to join their voices to honor Frank Sykes with the hymn, "Lift Every Voice and Sing." The final words of James Weldon Johnson's "Black National Anthem" are an invocation to the divine: "Shadowed beneath Thy hand, may we forever stand. True to our God, true to our native land." There could be no fitter epitaph to Frank Sykes's life, work, and legacy. He stayed true to the people and communities he loved throughout his life. His legacy is true and strong.

ENDNOTES

Preface

1 "Dr. Frank J. Sykes's 90th year: Celebration" (Howard University, July 24, 1982).

2 Charles Sykes, "Preface," email, August 18, 2023.

3 Bill Gibson, "Hear me talkin' to ya!" *Baltimore Afro-American,* August 5, 1933, 21. ProQuest Historical Newspapers: Black Newspapers.

4 "Doc Sykes," Negro Leagues Database, https://www.seamheads.com/NegroLgs/player.php?playerID=sykes01doc.

5 "American League Stars v. Baltimore Black Sox," *Baltimore Afro-American,* October 13, 1922, 11. ProQuest Historical Newspapers: Black Newspapers.

6 Telegram from Albert Einstein. Thomas Mann, et al. to Gov. Benjamen Meek Miller, https://scottsboroboysletters.as.ua.edu; "To See Justice Done": Letters from the Scottsboro Boys Trials," University of Alabama, Digital Humanities Center.

7 Robert G. O'Meally, "'Game to the Heart': Sterling Brown and the badman," *Callaloo* 14/15 (February-March 1982): 46.

Chapter 1

1 "Black Sox Bow Low," *Baltimore Sun*, May 14, 1923, 20. Newspapers.com.

2 "We Are Deeply and Profoundly Sorry," *Baltimore Sun*, February 18, 2022. https://www.baltimoresun.com/opinion/editorial/bs-ed-0220-sun-racial-reckoning-apology-online-20220218-qp32uybk5bgqrcnd732aicrouu-story.html.

3 Jeff Haby, "Weather and Baseball Flight," https://www.theweatherprediction.com/habyhints/285/.

4 "Black Sox and Giants Meet," *Baltimore Sun*, September 10, 1922, 19. Newspapers.com.

5 "Sam Streeter," Negro Leagues Database, https://www.seamheads.com/NegroLgs/player.php?playerID=stree01sam.

6 "Nate Johnson," Negro Leagues Database, https://www.seamheads.com/NegroLgs/player.php?playerID=johns01nat.

7 "Talmadge Richardson," Negro Leagues Database, https://www.seamheads.com/NegroLgs/player.php?playerID=richa01tal.

8 "Jud Wilson," Baseball Reference, https://www.baseball-reference.com/players/w/wilsoju99.shtml. "Black Sox," *Baltimore News*, September 11, 1922, 17. ProQuest Historical Newspapers.

9 Gibson, "Hear me talkin' to ya," 21.

10 "Sox Swamp Tigers," *Baltimore Afro-American*, June 3, 1921, 2; "Twin Bill to Black Sox," *Baltimore Afro-American*, October 14, 1921, 9. ProQuest Historical Newspapers: Black Newspapers.

11 "Doc Sykes Was a Pitcher and a Fighter Against Bigotry," *Baltimore Sun*, April 30, 1990, 21. Newspapers.com.

12 Craig Murder, "Dreyfuss Led Spitballer Ban," accessed June 12, 2020, https://baseballhall.org/discover/inside-pitch/dreyfuss-led-charge-to-ban-spitballers#:~:text=Contents&text=Barney%20Dreyfuss'%20greatest%20baseball%20legacy,ban%20all%20new%20spitball%20pitchers.

13 Gibson, "Hear me talkin' to ya," 21.

14 "Doc Sykes," Negro Leagues Database, https://www.seamheads.com/NegroLgs/player.php?playerID=sykes01doc.

15 Negro Baseball League, "Doc Sykes."

16 "Wheeler Allows One Hit until Eighth," *Morning News* (Wilmington), June 29, 1922, 9. Newspapers.com.

17 "White People Should Stay in Their Places," *Baltimore Afro-American*, October 20, 1922, 1. ProQuest Historical Newspapers: Black Newspapers. For Moton's views on segregation, see https://encyclopediavirginia.org/entries/moton-robert-russa-1867-1940/.

18 C. M. Gibbs, "The SUNdial," *Baltimore Sun*, October 28, 1930, 14. Newspapers.com.

19 "Twin Bill to Black Sox," *Baltimore Afro-American*, October 14, 1921, 9. ProQuest Historical Newspapers: Black Newspapers.

20 "Black Sox," *Baltimore Afro-American*, October 13, 1922, 11. ProQuest Historical Newspapers: Black Newspapers.

21 Maryland Park, as it was constructed in 1920, could seat about 7,000 to 8,000 spectators. After the 1922 season, in anticipation of play in the Eastern Colored League, the Black Sox added additional seating for a capacity of 12,000-14,000. See Bernard McKenna's *The Baltimore Black Sox* (McFarland, 2020), 80-81 and 96-97.

22 "Weather," *Baltimore Sun*, October 15, 1922, 27. Newspapers.com.

23 "Sykes Blanks All-Star Nine," *Baltimore Afro-American*, October 10, 1922, 11. ProQuest Historical Newspapers: Black Newspapers.

24 "Big Leaguers Shut Out by Black Sox," *Baltimore American*, October 16, 1922, 7. ProQuest Historical Newspapers.

25 "Big Leaguers Shut Out by Black Sox."

26 Gibson, "Hear me talkin' to ya," 21.

Chapter 2

1 Bill Glauber, "Doc Sykes Was a Pitcher and a Fighter against Bigotry," *Baltimore Sun*, April 30, 1990, 21. Newspapers.com.

2 "Decatur Dentist Says, 'Air Still Hot in Alabama Town,'" *Norfolk Journal and Guide*, May 6, 1933, 8. ProQuest Historical Newspapers: Black Newspapers.

3 "Guard Negroes after Assault on White Girls," *Chattanooga Daily Times*, March 26, 1931, 1. Newspapers.com.

4 "Girls from Huntsville," *Chattanooga Daily Times*, March 26, 1931, 2. Newspapers.com.

5 "Girls from Huntsville."

6 "Nine Blacks Outrage Two White Girls," *The Antlers American* (Oklahoma), April 2, 1931, 3. Newspapers.com.

7 "Girls from Huntsville."

8 "Cold Weather Prevents Lynching," *Philadelphia Tribune*, April 2, 1931, 14. ProQuest Historical Newspapers: Black Newspapers.

9 "Prisoners Moved as National Guard Is Withdrawn," *Norfolk Journal and Guide* (Norfolk, Virginia), April 4, 1931, 2. ProQuest Historical Newspapers: Black Newspapers.

10 "8,000 Whites at Georgia Rape Trial," *Baltimore Afro-American*, April 11, 1931, 19. ProQuest Historical Newspapers: Black Newspapers. Note: The headline misstated the location as Georgia rather than Alabama.

11 "Nine Alabama Men Saved from Lynchers," *Chicago Defender*, April 4, 1921, 1. ProQuest Historical Newspapers: Black Newspapers.

12 "Condemned Boys Write Pitiful Letters to Parents," *Norfolk Journal and Guide*, April 25, 1931, 5. ProQuest Historical Newspapers: Black Newspapers.

13 "Condemned Boys Write Pitiful Letters to Parents."

14 "Condemned Boys Write Pitiful Letters to Parents."

15 "Dr. Sykes Shakes Alabama Dust and Makes Home in Baltimore," *Baltimore Afro-American*, January 8, 1938, 24. ProQuest Historical Newspapers: Black Newspapers.

16 "Dr. Sykes Shakes Alabama Dust and Makes Home in Baltimore."

17 "Scottsboro Trial Goes into Second Week," *Baltimore*

Afro-American, April 8, 1933, 12. ProQuest Historical Newspapers: Black Newspapers.

18 "Defense ahead in Decatur Trial Now," *Baltimore Afro-American*, April 8, 1933, 2; "Scottsboro Boy Battles Chair," *New York Amsterdam News*, April 5, 1933, 1. ProQuest Historical Newspapers: Black Newspapers.

19 "The Air Is Still a Little Hot," *Norfolk Journal and Guide*, May 6, 1033, 18. ProQuest Historical Newspapers: Black Newspapers.

20 "Ku Klux Klan on Rampage in Alabama," *Baltimore Afro-American*, April 29, 1933, 13. ProQuest Historical Newspapers: Black Newspapers.

21 "Jury Ban Lifted in South," *Norfolk Journal and Guide*, April 13, 1935, 1. ProQuest Historical Newspapers: Black Newspapers.

22 "New York Greets Scottsboro Youths," *Philadelphia Tribune*, July 29, 1937, 1. ProQuest Historical Newspapers: Black Newspapers.

23 "Unknown Hero of the Scottsboro Case Praised," *Chicago Defender*, August 7, 1937, 1. ProQuest Historical Newspapers: Black Newspapers.

24 "Harlem Hails Four Scottsboro Boys," *Baltimore Afro-American*, July 31, 1937, 1. ProQuest Historical Newspapers: Black Newspapers.

25 "New Attack Begun on Alabama Juries," *Evening Sun* (Baltimore), March 30, 1933, 6. Newspapers.com.

26 Benjamin Quarles, "Justice Down in Dixie," *Baltimore Sun*, February 23, 1969, 91. Newspapers.com.

27 Dan Carter, *Scottsboro: A Tragedy of the American South* (Baton Rouge: Louisiana State University Press, 2007), 201.

28 Peggy Allen Towns, *Scottsboro Unmasked: Decatur's Story* (Author's House, 2018): 7.

29 Sheryll Cashin, *The Agitator's Daughter: A Memoir of Four Generations of One Extraordinary African American Family* (New York: Public Affairs, 2008), 75.

30 Glauber, "Doc Sykes Was a Pitcher and a Fighter against Bigotry," 21.

Chapter 3

1 Peggy Allen Towns, *Scapegoat: The Tommy Lee Hines Story* (Author House, 2020): 7.

2 John N. Ingham, "Building Businesses, Creating Communities: Residential Segregation and the Growth of African American Business in Southern Cities, 1880–1915," *Business History Review* 77, no. 4 (2003): 639.

3 Archie Snowden, "Old Town in Decatur Serves as Forgotten African American History," News 19 (Huntsville, AL), February 10, 2023, https://whnt.com/community/black-history-month/old-town-in-decatur-serves-as-forgotten-african-american-history/.

4 Brian Corrigan, "Decatur's Old Town Holds Community Stories," Muscle Shoals National Heritage Area, December 7, 2022, https://msnha.una.edu/decaturs-old-town-holds-community-stories/.

5 "Towns is passionate about history. She's turned that passion into three books on the subject, including the impact African Americans had during the Civil War. Towns says Decatur was home to the first of only two black regiments in Alabama in the Civil War. 'They were called United States Colored Infantry Regiment. So, Decatur has the distinction of raising the first, there were only two, in the entire state of Alabama.'" "Black History Month: Pioneers of Freedom from Decatur," WAFF 48 (Huntsville, AL), https://www.waff.com/2022/02/26/black-history-month-pioneers-freedom-decatur/.

6 Snowden, "Old Town."

7 Corrigan, "Decatur's Old Town."

8 Deangelo McDaniel, "Rare Decatur Hospital Photo Found in California Library," Tuscaloosanews.com, October 15, 2018, https://www.tuscaloosanews.com/story/news/state/2018/10/15/rare-decatur-hospital-photo-found-in-california-library/9547728007/.

9 McDaniel, "Rare Decatur Hospital Photo Found in California Library."

10 Decatur-Morgan County Chamber of Commerce, "Black History Month Spotlight," February 15, 2023, https://www.dcc.

org/2023/02/15/59124/.

11 W. E. Sterrs, "Wounds of Carotid Artery: Reports of Two Cases," *Journal of the National Medical Association* 4, no. 1 (1912): 42.

12 John A. Kenney, "Some Facts Concerning Negro Nurse Training Schools and Their Graduates," *Journal of the National Medical Association* 11, no. 2 (1919): 54.

13 Decatur-Morgan County Chamber of Commerce, "Spotlight."

14 "A River Runs Through Alabama Artist Frances Tate's Paintings," Alabama News Center, March 10, 2023, https://www.alabamanewscenter.com/2023/03/10/a-river-runs-through-alabama-artist-frances-tates-paintings/.

15 Ingham, "Building Businesses, Creating Communities," 665.

16 Snowden, "Old Town."

17 The 1900 census suggests that there may have been an older child who no longer lived with the family. The census records that Solomon and Ada had ten children, with seven surviving. In 1900, the Sykes family had only five children. Unfortunately, 1890 census data is unavailable. US Census Bureau, Year: 1900; Census Place: Decatur, Morgan, Alabama; Roll: 35; Page: 11; Enumeration District: 0124.

18 US Census Bureau, Year: 1900.

19 James D. Anderson, *The Education of Blacks in the South, 1860-1935* (Chapel Hill: University of North Carolina Press, 1988): 5.

20 Anderson, *The Education of Blacks in the South*, 31.

21 Dale Cohen, Sheida White, and Steffaney B. Cohen, "Mind the Gap: The Black-White Literacy Gap in the National Assessment of Adult Literacy and Its Implications," *Journal of Literary Research* 44, no. 2 (2012): 125.

22 Carolyn M. Moehling, "Family Structure, School Attendance, and Child Labor in the American South in 1900 and 1910," *Explorations in Economic History* 41, no. 1 (January 2004): 86, 89, and 94.

23 US Census Bureau, Year: 1900; Census Place: Decatur, Morgan, Alabama; Roll: 35; Page: 11; Enumeration District: 0124. Year: 1910;

Census Place: Decatur, Morgan, Alabama; Roll: T624_29; Page: 23b; Enumeration District: 0147; FHL microfilm: 1374042.

24 Alabama, United States County Marriage Records, 1805-1967.

25 "1860 Lawrence County Slave Schedule," transcribed by Charity Goodwin and Pat Sparks, February 6, 2001, https://sites.rootsweb.com/~allawren/census/1860Slave.htm.

26 William Jones, "Scottsboro Witness Product of Old South—Mother Colored, Father White," *Baltimore Afro-American*, April 8, 1933, 1.ProQuest Historical Newspapers: Black Newspapers.

27 "Swopes Lacey Family Tree," https://www.ancestrylibrary.com/family-tree/person/tree/67967906/person/120134720010/story.

28 "For Representative," *Moulton Democrat* (Moulton, Alabama), July 5, 1855, 3. Newspapers.com.

29 "The Greenbackers," *Clark County Democrat* (Grove Hill, Alabama), August 10, 1877, 1. Newspapers.com.

30 "Hon. F. W. Sykes," *Alabama Courier*, January 11, 1883, 3. Newspapers.com.

31 Jones, "Scottsboro Witness Product of Old South," 1.

32 "Christmas Carousels," *New Decatur Advertiser*, December 27, 1890, 3. Newspapers.com.

33 "Negro Found Dead Under Suspicious Circumstances," *Birmingham Post Herald*, November 29, 1900, 6. Newspapers.com.

34 "Policeman Roberson Cut," *New Decatur Advertiser*, October 27, 1899, 2. Newspapers.com.

35 E. C. Moore, "The Social Value of the Saloon," *The American Journal of Sociology* 3, no. 1 (July 1897): 4.

36 Jon M. Kingsdale, "The 'Poor Man's Club': Social Functions of the Urban Working-Class Saloon," *American Quarterly* 25, no. 4 (Oct. 1973): 472.

37 "The Mass Meeting," *The Alabama Enquirer*, June 14, 1888, 5. Newspapers.com.

38 Cullman Tribune, "Morgan County," August 23, 1888, 4.

39 "Disastrous Fire in New Decatur," *Birmingham Post Herald*, April 19, 1900, 3. Newspapers.com.

40 "Sol Sykes," *Birmingham Post Herald*, October 29, 1900, 3. Newspapers.com.

41 "Sunday Was a Bay," *The Decatur Weekly News*, October 5, 1900, 5. Newspapers.com.

42 "Local News," *New Decatur Advertiser*, December 1, 1900, 5. Newspapers.com.

43 "With the Merchants," *New Decatur Advertiser*, December 21, 1900, 7. Newspapers.com.

Chapter 4

1 "The N.A.A.C.P.," *The Crisis* 1, no. 1 (November 1910): 12.

2 "Editorial," *The Crisis* 1, no. 1 (November 1910): 10.

3 "Economic," *The Crisis* 1, no. 1 (November 1910): 6.

4 "Education," *The Crisis* 1, no. 1 (November 1910): 4.

5 Benjamin Griffith Brawley, "The Prisoner at the Bar," *The Atlanta Constitution,* June 19, 1910, 3. Newspapers.com.

6 "Atlanta Baptist College," *The New York Age*, July 20, 2011, 3. ProQuest Historical Newspapers: Black Newspapers.

7 Glenn Sisk, "Section D: Morehouse College," *Journal of Negro Education* 27, no. 2 (Spring 1955): 201.

8 Benjamin Griffith Brawley, *History of Morehouse College written on the authority of the Board of Trustees* (Atlanta: Morehouse College, 1917): 17.

9 Sisk, "Section D: Morehouse College," 202.

10 W. E. B Du Bois, *Du Bois: Essays: The Black North, Of the Training of Black Men, The Talented Tenth, The Conservation of Races* (Chicago: Musaicum Books, 2018).

11 James D. Anderson, *The Education of Blacks in the South* (Chapel Hill: University of North Carolina Press, 1980): 3, 1.

12 Jelani M. Favors, *Shelter in a Time of Storm: How Black Colleges Fostered Generations of Leadership and Activism* (Chapel Hill: University of North Carolina Press, 2019): 5.

13 Brawley, *History of Morehouse College*, 106.

14 Sisk, "Section D: Morehouse College," 201.

15 Thomas H. Martin, *Atlanta and Its Builders: A Comprehensive History of the Gate City of the Sea* (Boston: Century Memorial Publishing Company, 1902): 313-314.

16 Brawley, *History of Morehouse College*, 85-86 and 107.

17 Brawley, History of Morehouse College, 127.

18 "Prominent Speakers at Negro Mass Meeting," *The Atlanta Constitution,* January 27, 1910, 7. Newspapers.com.

19 Brawley, *History of Morehouse College*, 129-130.

20 Bill Glauber of the *Baltimore Sun* wrote that Sykes attended Atlanta Baptist College for only one year, but evidence from other sources suggests that he was there for two years (1910-1911 and 1911-1912).

21 "Intercollegiate Games," *The Atlanta Constitution*, March 30, 1912: 8. Newspapers.com.

22 Layton Revel and Louis Munoz, *Forgotten Heroes: Dick "Cannonball" Redding* (Carrolton, Texas: Center for Negro League Baseball Research, 2013): 34.

23 "Atlanta Dephins Play Atlanta Baptist College," *The Atlanta Journal Constitution*, March 22, 1911, 10. Newspapers.com.

24 Glauber, "Doc Sykes Was a Pitcher and Fighter Against Bigotry," 21.

25 Robert Logan, *Howard University: The First Hundred Years, 1867-1967* (New York: New York University Press, 1969): 163.

26 "Georgetown University," *Sunday Star*, September 22, 1912, 75. Newspapers.com.

27 John W. Parker, "Benjamin Brawley and the American Cultural Tradition," *Phylon* 16, no. 2 (1955): 183.

28 Benjamin Griffith Brawley, *The Negro in Literature and Art in the United States* (New York: Duffield and Company, 1921): 7-8.

29 William H. Taft, *Presidential Address and State Papers* (New York: Doubleday, Page, and Company, 1910): 111-112.

30 Logan, *Howard University*, 15.

31 Logan, *Howard University*, 156.

32 "Royal Welcome for Dr. Stephen Morrell Newman," the *Pittsburgh Courier*, December 27, 1912, 1. ProQuest Historical Newspapers: Black Newspapers.

33 "Brooklyn Giants Win," *The Washington Herald*, May 8, 1913, 8. Newspapers.com.

34 "Sports and Athletics," *Baltimore Afro-American*, May 2, 1914, 4. ProQuest Historical Newspapers: Black Newspapers; "Giants Looked Like Pigmies," *The Daily Star* (Fredericksburg, VA), 2. Newspapers.com.

35 "Howard 4, Morris Brown 1," *The Atlanta Constitution*, April 10, 1916, 8. Newspapers.com.

36 "Dedication of Carnegie Library," *Howard University Record* 4, no. 2 (March 1910): 16.

37 "President Taft Condemns Lynching," *Franklin's Paper the Statesman* (Denver, CO), May 4, 1912, 5.

38 "Taft Denounces Lynching," *National League of Negroes*, May 2, 1912, 1.

39 "Lynchers Should Banged," *Baltimore Afro-American*, April 13, 1912, 1. ProQuest Historical Newspapers: Black Newspapers.

40 "Dedication of Carnegie Library," 17.

41 "Editorial," *The Crisis* 1, no. 1 (November 1910): 11.

Chapter 5

1 "The Prince and Thou, A to Z Paupers," *Baltimore Afro-American*, May 3, 1975, 9. ProQuest Historical Newspapers: Black Newspapers.

2 "Beating the Gun," the *Philadelphia Tribune*, December 19, 1950, 10. ProQuest Historical Newspapers: Black Newspapers.

3 Robert Peterson, *Only the Ball Was White: A History of Legendary Black Players and All-Black Professional Teams* (New York: Oxford University Press, 1970): 63.

4 Mark Ribowsky, *A Complete History of the Negro Leagues* (New York: Birch Lane Press, 1995): 81-82.

5 "Big Plans ahead for Colored Teams," *The Brooklyn Daily Eagle*, February 9, 1911, 26. Newspapers.com.

6 "Baseball Season Opens," *The New York Age*, April 9, 1914, 6. Newspapers.com.

7 "Break Even in Four Games," *The New York Age*, June 4, 1914, 6. Newspapers.com.

8 "Royal Giants Twice Defeat the Lincolns," *The Brooklyn Daily Eagle*, July 5, 1914, 26. Newspapers.com.

9 "Royals Even Series with Lincolns," *The New York Age*, July 9, 1914, 6. Newspapers.com.

10 "Giants Win another," *The Brooklyn Daily Eagle*, July 11, 1914, 18. Newspapers.com.

11 "At Olympic Field," *The Standard Review*, July 13, 1914, 9. Newspapers.com.

12 Gary Ashwill, "Lincoln Stars in Cuba, 1914" in *Agate Type: Reconstructing Negro League and Latin American Baseball History*, October 1, 2006.

13 "Baseball," *Camden Post Telegram*, July 9, 1914, 11. Newspapers.com.

14 "Mid-Week Game at Uptown Ballpark," *Camden Post Telegram*, July 7, 1914, 8. Newspapers.com.

15 "Lincoln Stars to Play Kansas City," *Camden Daily Courier*, July 9, 1914, 11. Newspapers.com.

16 "Giants Begin Season Today," *Atlantic City Gazette Review*, July 18, 1914, 15. Newspapers.com.

17 "John W. Connor," *The Standard Union* (Brooklyn), April 17, 1904, 6. Newspapers.com.

18 "Amateur Baseball," *The Standard Union* (Brooklyn), May 14, 1904, 10. Newspapers.com.

19 "Baseball," *The Standard Union* (Brooklyn), June 5, 1902, 9; "James E. Brown," *The Standard Union* (Brooklyn), August 16, 1903, 6. Newspapers.com. The Colored Niantics may have their origins in

a team called the Niantic Athletic Club. See James E. Brunson, III, *Black Baseball, 1858-1900* (Jefferson, North Carolina: McFarland, 2019): 157.

20 "J. E. Boone," *The Standard Union* (Brooklyn), February 22, 1905, 6; "Royal Giants Beam," *The Brooklyn Citizen*, February 27, 1905, 6. Newspapers.com.

21 "Square Deal for Red Caps," *The New York Age*, June 8, 1918, 6. Newspapers.com.

22 "Baseball," *Atlantic City Gazette Review*, August 6, 1914, 13. Newspapers.com.

23 "Atlantic City in Great Exhibition," *Press of Atlantic City*, August 4, 1914, 7. Newspapers.com.

24 "Royal Giants Easy for Bushwick Nine," *The Brooklyn Daily Eagle*, August 10, 1914, 11. Newspapers.com.

25 "Brooklyn Royal Giants Defeat Clifton," *Delaware County Daily Times* (Chester, Pennsylvania), August 14, 1914, 7. Newspapers.com.

26 "Royal Giants Finally Defeat Bushwicks," *The Brooklyn Daily Eagle*, August 17, 1914, 15. Newspapers.com.

27 "Royal Giants Win in Newark," *The New York Age*, August 20, 1914, 6. Newspapers.com.

28 "Royal Giants 9 Capture 2," *Perth Amboy News*, August 21, 1914, 21; "Giants Show Them How," *The Philadelphia Inquirer*, August 23, 1914, 39; "Atlantic City Team Loses to Brooklyn," *Atlantic City Gazette Review*, August 25, 1914, 13. Newspapers.com.

29 "Camden City Pulled a Bunch of Boneheads," *Courier Post* (Camden), September 21, 1914, 11. Newspapers.com.

30 "Royal Giants Lose First Game," *The New York Age*, September 3, 1914, 6; "Royal Giants Defeat Philadelphia Giants," *The New York Age*, October 8, 1914, 6. Newspapers.com.

31 "American Giants Win Again," *Chicago Tribune*, September 8, 1914, 14. Newspapers.com.

32 Frank A. Young, "Americans Leading Lincoln," *Chicago Defender*,

August 7, 1915, 7. ProQuest Historical Newspapers: Black Newspapers.

33 "Champions at Ridgewood," *Times Union* (Brooklyn), June 4, 1915, 10. Newspapers.com.

34 "Baseball Games by Colored Teams," *The Courier* (Harrisburg, Pennsylvania), March 21, 1915, 5. Newspapers.com.

35 "Ridgewood Teams Beaten in Close Double Header," *The Brooklyn Daily Eagle*, May 3, 1915, 19; "Ridgewood Teams Lose," *Times Union* (Brooklyn), May 10, 1915, 4; "Fast Pitchers Battle Is Lost by Suburbans," May 24, 1915, 19. Newspapers.com.

36 "Lincoln Giants Win at Ridgewood," *The Brooklyn Daily Eagle*, June 6, 1915, 83. Newspapers.com.

37 "All Local Favorites," *Harrisburg Telegraph*, September 24, 1915, 13. Newspapers.com.

38 "The Brooklyn Royal Giants," *The Brooklyn Daily Eagle*, June 4, 1915, 15. Newspapers.com.

39 Ashwill, "Lincoln Stars in Cuba, 1914."

40 "East and West Will Battle at Camden City Park," *Courier Post* (Camden), August 18, 1915, 11. Newspapers.com.

41 "Cubans Lose to Lincoln Stars," *Asbury Park Press*, August 25, 1915, 3. Newspapers.com.

42 "Sykes Fans Sixteen as Lincoln Stars Lose," the *Chicago Defender*, September 11, 1915, 7. ProQuest Historical Newspapers: Black Newspapers.

43 "Cubans Receive Severe Beating," *Ashbury Park Press*, July 13, 1915, 10. Newspapers.com.

44 "Lincoln Stars Beat ABCs," the *Chicago Defender*, August 21, 1915, 7. ProQuest Historical Newspapers: Black Newspapers.

45 "Double Win for Lincoln Giants," *The Morning Post* (Camden), August 23, 1915, 9. Newspapers.com.

46 "American Giants on Top in Long Pitcher's Battle," *Chicago Defender*, August 14, 1915, 7. ProQuest Historical Newspapers: Black Newspapers.

47 Frank A. Young, "Jones Error Paves Way for Giants' Victory," *Chicago Defender*, May 27, 1922, 10. ProQuest Historical Newspapers: Black Newspapers.

Chapter 6

1 "Sykes," *The New York Age*, June 1, 1916, 8. Newspapers.com.

2 "War Department and Enlistment," *The New York Age*, June 1, 1916, 8. Newspapers.com.

3 Seamheads.com has his record with Lincoln as one win and nine losses, and with the Royal Giants as two wins and one loss.

4 "Oscar Charleston," Negro Leagues Database, https://www.seamheads.com/NegroLgs/player.php?playerID=charl01osc.

5 "New York Lincoln Stars, 1915" Negro Leagues Database, https://www.seamheads.com/NegroLgs/team.php?yearID=1915&teamID=NLS&LGOrd=1.

6 "New York Lincoln Stars, 1916," Negro Leagues Database, https://www.seamheads.com/NegroLgs/team.php?yearID=1916&teamID=NLS&LGOrd=1.

7 "Semi Pro Gossip," *The Brooklyn Daily Eagle*, May 13, 1916, 17. Newspapers.com.

8 "Brooklyn Royal Giants, 1916," Negro League Database, https://www.seamheads.com/NegroLgs/team.php?yearID=1916&teamID=BRG&LGOrd=1.

9 "Camden Defeated by Lincoln Stars," *The Morning Post* (Camden), June 5, 1916, 8. Newspapers.com.

10 "The Lennox Oval," *The Sun* (New York), July 3, 1916, 13. Newspapers.com.

11 "Baseball," *The New York Age*, July 20, 1916, 6. Newspapers.com.

12 "Gatewood Defeats the Lincoln Stars," the *Chicago Defender*, August 5, 1916, 7. ProQuest Historical Newspapers: Black Newspapers.

13 "Lincolns own Giants, 10-9," *The Chicago Tribune*, August 8, 1916,

9. Newspapers.com.

14 "Lincoln Stars Get a Double Defeat," the *Chicago Defender*, September 23, 1916,9 . ProQuest Historical Newspapers: Black Newspapers.

15 "Santop and Sykes Join Royal Giants," *The Standard Union* (Brooklyn), September 1, 1916, 8. Newspapers.com.

16 "Royal Giants Win Two Ball Games," *The Brooklyn Daily Eagle*, September 4, 1916, 11. Newspapers.com.

17 "Down Goes Millville," *Philadelphia Inquirer*, September 24, 1916, 58; Newspapers.com. "Royal Giants Win," the *Chicago Defender*, September 30, 1916, 4; ProQuest Historical Newspapers: Black Newspapers. "Baseball," *The New York Age*, October 19, 1916, 6. Newspapers.com.

18 "Two for Lincoln Giants," *Times Union* (Brooklyn), September 11, 1916, 9; "Redding Wins Two," *The Standard Union* (Brooklyn), September 11, 1916, 9. Newspapers.com.

19 Neil Lanctot, *Fair Dealing and Clean Playing: The Hilldale Club and the Development of Black Professional Baseball* (Syracuse: Syracuse University Press, 1994): 17.

20 "A Short History of Hilldale," *Philadelphia Tribune*, April 8, 1916, 7.

21 Lanctot, *Fair Dealing and Clean Playing*, 17. ProQuest Historical Newspapers: Black Newspapers.

22 "Bolden Named Chair of Eastern Colored League," *The New York Amsterdam News*, March 7, 1923, 4. ProQuest Historical Newspapers: Black Newspapers.

23 Lanctot, *Fair Dealing and Clean Playing*, 23.

24 "A Short History of Hilldale," 7.

25 Lanctot, *Fair Dealing and Clean Playing*, 23.

26 Michael Lomax, *Black Baseball Entrepreneurs, 1902-1931* (Syracuse, New York: Syracuse University Press, 2014): 192.

27 "Hilldale and Pitcher Sykes," *Philadelphia Tribune*, June 9, 1917, 7. ProQuest Historical Newspapers: Black Newspapers.

28 "Hilldale Lands Sykes," the *Chicago Defender*, June 16, 1917, 3.

ProQuest Historical Newspapers: Black Newspapers.

29 "Dramatics and Athletics," *The New York Age*, June 14, 1917, 6.

30 Lanctot, *Fair Dealing and Clean Playing*, 44. Newspapers.com.

31 "Hilldale Loses and Wins on Decoration Day," *Philadelphia Tribune*, June 9, 1917, 7. ProQuest Historical Newspapers: Black Newspapers.

32 Sykes also pitched a game for the Philadelphia Giants, losing two to zero ("Pergolas Down Colored Team," *The Allentown Democrat*, August 27, 1917, 6). Newspapers.com. "Seamheads Lists His Record for Hilldale as Four Wins and Four Losses," https://www.seamheads.com/NegroLgs/player.php?playerID=sykes01doc.

33 "Hilldale 11; Norristown Giants, 0," *Philadelphia Tribune*, June 2, 1917, 7. ProQuest Historical Newspapers: Black Newspapers.

34 "Hilldale Shuts Out Logan Square," *Philadelphia Tribune*, June 16, 1917, 7. ProQuest Historical Newspapers: Black Newspapers.

35 "Hilldale Downs Logan Square," *Philadelphia Tribune*, July 28, 1917, 7. ProQuest Historical Newspapers: Black Newspapers.

36 "Sykes Pitches for Hilldale," *Philadelphia Tribune*, August, 1917, 18. ProQuest Historical Newspapers: Black Newspapers.

37 "Hilldale Too Much for Wildwood," *Philadelphia Tribune*, September 29, 1917, 7. ProQuest Historical Newspapers: Black Newspapers.

38 "Hilldale Divides," *Philadelphia Tribune*, September 8, 1917, 7. ProQuest Historical Newspapers: Black Newspapers.

39 "Bacharach Giants Put Check to Hilldale's Streak," *Philadelphia Tribune*, June 22, 1917, 14. ProQuest Historical Newspapers: Black Newspapers.

40 "Hilldale Wins from Patterson and Lose to Cuban Stars," *Philadelphia Tribune*, July 7, 1917, 7. ProQuest Historical Newspapers: Black Newspapers.

41 "Hilldale Defeats Brooklyn Royal Giants, 9 to 1," *Philadelphia Tribune*, August 25, 1917, 7. ProQuest Historical Newspapers: Black Newspapers.

42 "Sykes Pitches Hilldales to Win over Brooklyn Royal Giants," the

Chicago Defender, August 25, 1917, 10. ProQuest Historical Newspapers: Black Newspapers.

43 "Hilldale Closes Successful Season," *Philadelphia Tribune*, October 27, 1917, 7. ProQuest Historical Newspapers: Black Newspapers.

44 "World War I Draft Registration Cards, 1917–1918," digital image, Ancestry.com, http://www.ancestry.com: accessed 10 July 2023. Frank Jehoy Sykes registration, no. 133 (right side numbering), Draft Board, City of Washington, DC; citing World War I Selective Service System Draft Registration Cards, 1917–1918.

45 "Sykes Called to Colors," *Philadelphia Tribune* July 6, 1912, 7. ProQuest Historical Newspapers: Black Newspapers.

46 Frank J. Sykes, U.S., Department of Veterans Affairs BIRLS Death File, 1850-2010.

47 Edward Bolden, "Hilldale on Edge for Opening Clash," *Philadelphia Tribune*, April 13, 1918, 7. ProQuest Historical Newspapers: Black Newspapers.

48 "Seamheads Lists His Record as Two Wins and Two Losses," https://www.seamheads.com/NegroLgs/player.php?playerID=sykes01doc.

49 "The Bacharach Giants Lose Exciting Game," the *Chicago Defender*, May 25, 1918, 9. ProQuest Historical Newspapers: Black Newspapers.

50 "Sports of All Sports: Hilldale Takes Another from Bacharachs, 8 -1," *Philadelphia Tribune*, May 25, 1918, 7. ProQuest Historical Newspapers: Black Newspapers.

51 "Hilldale Swamps Bacharach Giants," *The Philadelphia Inquirer*, June 21, 1918, 12. Newspapers.com.

52 "Hilldale Defeats Hog," *Philadelphia Tribune*, July 6, 1918, 7. ProQuest Historical Newspapers: Black Newspapers.

53 "Pennsylvania Giants Divide Double Header," *Philadelphia Tribune*, August 17, 1918, 7. ProQuest Historical Newspapers: Black Newspapers.

54 "Bacharach Giants Standing," *Atlantic City Gazette Review*, August 4, 1919, 7; "Farmers Add Red Caps to List of Victims," *The Standard*

Union (Brooklyn), August 24, 1919, 14. Newspapers.com.

55 "To Play Le Troit Tigers," the *Baltimore Sun*, April 16, 1920. Newspapers.com.

56 "Jackson on Rampage," the *New York Times*, June 1, 1916, 12. Newspapers.com.

57 "750 State Negroes Called to Service," *The Evening Journal* (Wilmington, Delaware), July 26, 1918, 13. Newspapers.com.

Chapter 7

1 Year: 1920; Census Place: Baltimore Ward 17, Baltimore (Independent City), Maryland; Roll: T625_663; Page: 10A; Enumeration District: 299.

2 "Up in Arms Against B & O Railroad," *Baltimore Afro-American*, February 3, 1912, 1. ProQuest Historical Newspapers: Black Newspapers.

3 "Dr. Young Expects All to Help," *Baltimore Afro-American*, Dec. 6, 1913, 1. ProQuest Historical Newspapers: Black Newspapers.

4 "Dr. Young Expects All to Help."

5 Sherry Olson, *Baltimore: The Building of an American City* (Baltimore: Johns Hopkins University Press, 1997), 375.

6 Garret Power, "Apartheid Baltimore Style: The Residential Segregation Ordinances of 1910- 1913," *Maryland Law Review* 42, no. 2 (October 2012): 289-290.

7 "A Big Surprise," *The Chicago Whip*, March 27, 1920, 5. Newspapers.com.

8 Seamheads records one win and one loss, "Frank Sykes," https://www.seamheads.com/NegroLgs/player.php?playerID=sykes01doc.

9 The *Baltimore Sun* lists him as the scheduled starter in two games: "To Play Le Droit Tigers," *Baltimore Sun*, April 16, 1920, 12; "Norfolks to Visit Black Sox," *Baltimore Sun*, June 5, 1920, 8. The *Evening Sun* lists him as the starting pitcher in another game: "Black Sox to Busy," The *Evening Sun* (Baltimore), June 11, 1920, 27. Newspapers.com.

10 "Charlie Thomas," *Baltimore Afro-American*, August 20, 1920, 7.

ProQuest Historical Newspapers: Black Newspapers.

11 "Black Sox Divide Sunday," *Baltimore Afro-American*, September 3, 1920, 7. ProQuest Historical Newspapers: Black Newspapers.

12 "Fellows, Here's the Grand Old Game," *The Evening Journal* (Wilmington, Delaware), September 16, 1920, 9; "Black Sox Win First of Series," *The Evening Journal* (Wilmington, Delaware), September 21, 1920, 13; "Hilldale Wins; One Hit for Black Sox," *The Evening Journal* (Wilmington, Delaware), September 28, 1920, 13; "Hilldale Wins Another," *The Philadelphia Inquirer*, September 28, 1920, 14. Newspapers.om.

13 "Black Sox Plan Beason," *Baltimore Afro-American*, February 25, 1921, 7. ProQuest Historical Newspapers: Black Newspapers.

14 "Black Sox Open Season With Victory 7 to 1," *Baltimore Afro-American*, April 15, 1921, 5; "Sykes on Mound Beats Cubans in Twelve-Inning Game," *Philadelphia Tribune*, July 5, 1924, 9. ProQuest Historical Newspapers: Black Newspapers.

15 "Rexmen Split Even," *Washington Herald*, May 16, 1921, 6; Newspapers.com. "Baltimore Sox Split Even," the *Chicago Defender*, May 21, 1921, 4. ProQuest Historical Newspapers: Black Newspapers.

16 "Black Sox Lose Both," *Baltimore Afro-American*, September 23, 1921, 9. ProQuest Historical Newspapers: Black Newspapers.

17 "Parksides Lose Two Sunday," *The Morning News* (Wilmington, Delaware), June 13, 1921, 8; Newspapers.com."Baltimore Sox Divide," the *Chicago Defender*, June 11, 1921, 10. ProQuest Historical Newspapers: Black Newspapers.

18 "Baltimore Sox, Subbing for Bacharach Giants, Surprise Hilldale Crew," *Camden Daily Courier* (Camden, New Jersey), September 15, 1921, 16. Newspapers.com.

19 "Black Sox Win over Hilldale," *Baltimore Afro-American*, July 21, 1922, 6. ProQuest Historical Newspapers: Black Newspapers.

20 "Armstrong Manual Training School," *Evening Star* (Washington, DC), May 28, 1922, 26. Newspapers.com.

21 "Black Sox Make It Twelve Straight," *Baltimore Afro-American*, June 30, 1922, 9. ProQuest Historical Newspapers: Black Newspapers.

22 "Black Sox Incorporate," *Baltimore Afro-American*, July 29, 1921, 2. ProQuest Historical Newspapers: Black Newspapers.

23 "Sykes, the Black Sox Best Pitcher," the *Gazette and Daily Record* (York, Pennsylvania), September 19, 1922, 7. Newspapers.com.

24 "Black Sox Had Great Season," *Baltimore Afro-American*, December 8, 1922, 7. ProQuest Historical Newspapers: Black Newspapers.

25 Randall Cassell, "A Win for the Black Sox Nine Means a Challenge from a Strong Rival—Pennsylvania Becomes Stomping Ground," the *Evening Sun*, August 11, 1922, 17. Newspapers.com.

26 "Black Sox Drop Two Hot Contests," *Baltimore Afro-American*, June 9, 1922, 9. ProQuest Historical Newspapers: Black Newspapers.

27 "Sox Sign Catcher and New Pitchers," *Baltimore Afro-American*, February 9, 1923, 11. ProQuest Historical Newspapers: Black Newspapers.

28 "9,000 Fans Saw Black Sox and Bacharachs Divide Sunday," *Baltimore Afro-American*, May 11, 1923, 14. ProQuest Historical Newspapers: Black Newspapers.

29 "Five Homers Feature in Sunday's Twin Bill," *Baltimore Afro-American*, May 18, 1923, 15; "Sox Play Hilldale in the Eastern Colored League," *Baltimore Afro-American*, May 25, 1923, 14; "Sykes Lost This One," *Baltimore Afro-American*, June 1, 1923, 14; "Stars Down into Third Place Last Sunday," *Baltimore Afro-American*, June 8, 1923, 14. ProQuest Historical Newspapers: Black Newspapers.

30 "Washington Potomacs Show Class in First Appearance before 4,000 Fans," *Baltimore Afro-American*, June 29, 1923, 14; "Bacharach Giants Shove Sox Further Down in Eastern League Pennant Race," *Baltimore Afro-American*, July 20, 1923, 14. ProQuest Historical Newspapers: Black Newspapers.

31 "Rain Ends Downfall," *Baltimore Afro-American*, August 10, 1923, 14. ProQuest Historical Newspapers: Black Newspapers.

32 "Sports," *Baltimore Afro-American*, August 17, 1923, 1. ProQuest Historical Newspapers: Black Newspapers.

33 "Hilldale Wins Four in a Row from Bacharachs," *Pittsburgh Courier*, August 25, 1923, 6. ProQuest Historical Newspapers: Black Newspapers.

34 "To My Patients and Friends," *Baltimore Afro-American*, September 7, 1923, 2; "Spedden Will 'Junk' Present Black Sox Club," *Baltimore Afro-American*, November 2, 1923, A15. ProQuest Historical Newspapers: Black Newspapers.

35 "Sykes Not Suspended," *Baltimore Afro-American*, January 11, 1924, 14. ProQuest Historical Newspapers: Black Newspapers.

36 "Blackmon Wins Twelve-Inning Game by Six Inches," *Baltimore Afro-American*, July 4, 1924, 15. ProQuest Historical Newspapers: Black Newspapers.

37 "Doc Sykes Is Released," *Baltimore Afro-American*, August 1, 1924, 14. ProQuest Historical Newspapers: Black Newspapers; *New Journal and Guide* (Norfolk, Virginia), August 9, 1924, 4. Newspapers.com.

38 Louise Camphor, "'Doc' Sykes Leaves for Decatur, Alabama," *Baltimore Afro-American*, March 27, 1926, 8. ProQuest Historical Newspapers: Black Newspapers.

Chapter 8

1 "The Weather," *The Montgomery Advertiser* (Montgomery, Alabama), October 11, 1925, 1; "Rising Mercury Seen for Sunday," *The Birmingham News* (Birmingham, Alabama), October 11, 1925, 1; "Albany Policemen Held for Murder," *The Birmingham News* (Birmingham, Alabama), November 8, 1925, 1; "Preliminary Trial of Two Policemen Postponed Today," *The Albany Decatur Daily Record*, November 10, 1925, 1; "Judge Lowe Today Conducts Hearing for Two Policemen," *The Albany Decatur Daily Record*, November 16, 1925, 1. Newspapers.com.

2 "Decision in Two Officer's Cases Expected Soon," the *Albany Decatur Daily Record*, November 17, 1925, 1; "Stewart Allowed Bond, but West Is Remanded to Jail," the *Albany Decatur Daily Record*, November 18, 1925, 1; "Lawyers Present Arguments over West Case Status," the *Albany Decatur Daily Record*, February 16, 1926, 1; "Woman's Charge to Be Heard Sunday," the *Albany Decatur Daily Record*, April 16, 1926, 1; "Affirmation of West Case Given," the *Decatur Daily*, May 25, 1927, 1; "West Is Here," the *Decatur Daily*, August 8, 1927, 8; "West Pleas Denied by Highest Court," the *Decatur Daily*, October 22, 1927, 1; "Sees Good Team," the *Decatur Daily*, December 14, 1927, 6; "Strong Appeals for West's Parole," the *Montgomery Advertiser* (Montgomery, Alabama), January 12, 1928, 12; "Alabama News In Brief," *Weekly Call* (Birmingham, Alabama), January 14, 1928, 1; "Parole to West Denied by Board," the *Decatur Daily*, January 30, 1928, 4; "Monroe West Granted Parole by Graves on Eve of His Sentence," the *Decatur Daily*, January 31, 1928, 1; David Chalmers, "The Ku Klux Klan in Politics in the 1920's," the *Mississippi Quarterly* 18, 4 (Fall 1965): 237. Newspapers.com.

3 "Scottsboro Witness," the *Northwest Enterprise* (Seattle, Washington), May 4, 1933, 1. Newspapers.com.

4 "Well-Known Negro Dies of Pneumonia," the *Albany-Decatur Daily*, May 4, 1925, 1. Newspapers.com.

5 Dorothy Autrey, "Can These Bones Love?", the *National Association for the Advancement of Colored People in Alabama, 1918-1930*, 82, 1 (Winter 1997): 1.

6 W. Rollo Wilson, "Eastern Snapshot," the *Pittsburgh Courier*, July 31, 1926, 15. ProQuest Historical Newspapers: Black Newspapers.

7 Frank Sykes, Year: 1930; Census Place: Decatur, Morgan, Alabama; Page: 23A; Enumeration District: 0003; FHL microfilm: 2339779.

8 Alice West, Year: 1920; Census Place: Thornbury, Delaware, Pennsylvania; Roll: T625_1563; Page: 5A; Enumeration District: 203; "Big Brother Treat of Ten," Baltimore Afro-American, January 17, 1925,

7;"Tendered Shower," Baltimore Afro-American, June 19, 1926, 9. ProQuest Historical Newspapers: Black Newspapers.

9 Bill Gibson, "Hear Malkin' to Ya!", 21.

10 "National Dental Group Closes DC Meet," the *Chicago Defender*, August 21, 1937, 5; "Bermuda Dentist Among 280 from 24 States at Meet," *Baltimore Afro-American*, August 14, 1937, 9. ProQuest Historical Newspapers: Black Newspapers.

11 "Social News and Activities," *The Birmingham Reporter*, November 11, 1932, 5; "Social News and activities," *The Birmingham Reporter*, March 1, 1930, 2. Newspapers.com.

12 "Dr. Sykes Shakes Alabama Dust and Makes Home in Baltimore."

13 "New Crane Shows Value," *Baltimore Sun*, September 18, 1930, 10. Newspapers.com.

14 "Grain Shipments Revive," *Baltimore Sun*, July 25, 1938, 16; "Metal Exports Increased by Far East War," *Baltimore Sun*, August 21, 1937, 22; "Sailings with Cargo for Far East Fixture of Export Trade," *Baltimore Sun*, March 14, 1939, 23; "Grain Shipments from Baltimore Continue," *Baltimore Sun*, February 8, 1938, 19. Newspapers.com.

15 "South Baltimore," *Baltimore Sun*, November 24, 1939, 9; "Western Maryland RR Erects New Tracks," *Baltimore Sun*, December 10, 1939, 7; "Real Estate News and Building Deals," *Baltimore Sun*, October 18, 1939, 25. Newspapers.com.

16 "Miller Says DuBois No Longer Eats Fire," *Baltimore Afro-American*, January 8, 1938, 22. ProQuest Historical Newspapers: Black Newspapers.

17 "Pennsy to Punish Jim Crow Cabbies," *Baltimore Afro-American*, January 8, 1938, 20. ProQuest Historical Newspapers: Black Newspapers.

18 "Calvert County Grants Equal Teacher Salaries," *Baltimore Afro-American*, January 8, 1938,24. ProQuest Historical Newspapers: Black Newspapers.

19 "8 Lynchings in '37, No Arrests," *Baltimore Afro-American*, January

8, 1938, 7; "White Café Owner Wouldn't Serve Two," *Baltimore Afro-American*, January 8, 1938, 7. ProQuest Historical Newspapers: Black Newspapers.

20 Lillian Johnson, "What Is Happening to Us in the Theatre," *Baltimore Afro-American*, January 8, 1938, 11. ProQuest Historical Newspapers: Black Newspapers.

21 George Murphy, "Kids'll Love Him, but the Ladies . . . ," *Baltimore Afro-American*, January 8, 1938, 1-2. ProQuest Historical Newspapers: Black Newspapers.

22 Frank Sykes, Year: 1940; Census Place: Baltimore, Baltimore City, Maryland; Roll: m-t0627-01512; Page: 1B; Enumeration District: 4-140.

23 Frank Sykes, National Archives at Washington, DC; Washington, D.C.; Seventeenth Census of the United States, 1950; Year: 1950; Census Place: Baltimore, Maryland; Roll: 2112; Page: 1; Enumeration District: 4-427.

24 Dentist Entering Dance Hall Held Up by 6 Thugs," *Baltimore Afro-American*, February 14, 1942; "N.W. Baltimore Terrorists Draw Stiff Prison Terms," *Baltimore Afro American*, April 4, 1942. ProQuest Historical Newspapers: Black Newspapers.

25 "Elimination of Free Exams Proposed at Dental Conference," *Baltimore Afro-American*, October 19, 1946, 19. ProQuest Historical Newspapers: Black Newspapers.

26 "Raise Every Voice," *Baltimore Afro-American*, March 1, 1949, 9. ProQuest Historical Newspapers: Black Newspapers.

27 Sam Lacy, "From A to Z," *Baltimore Afro-American*, July 7, 1951, 16. ProQuest Historical Newspapers: Black Newspapers.

28 "Today's Weather," the *Baltimore Sun*, November 10, 1986, 56. Newspapers.com.

29 "Jocobsen Comes Home to Joyous Family," the *Baltimore Sun*, November 10, 1986, 1; A. Lin Neumann, "Aquino Appeals to Allies," the *Baltimore Sun*, November 10, 1986, 1; John Woodruff, "China

Increasingly Looks to U.S. to Upgrade Military," the *Baltimore Sun*, November 10, 1986, 1. Newspapers.com.

30 "U.S. Team Takes Finale in Japan, 9 -4," the *Baltimore Sun*, November 10, 1986, 35. Newspapers.com.

31 "Finding of Bias against Tandy Corp. Reversed on Appeal," the *Baltimore Sun*, November 10, 1986, 44. Newspapers.com.

32 Glauber, "Doc Sykes as a Pitcher and a Fighter Against Bigotry," 21.

Chapter 9

1 Glauber, "Doc Sykes was a pitcher and fighter against bigotry," 21.

2 "Frank 'Doc' Sykes," Baseball Reference, https://www.baseball-reference.com/players/s/sykesdo01.shtml.

3 James Brady, "A Historic Legacy Nearly Gone," September 9, 1999, 67.

4 "Exhibit Looks at Blacks in Baseball in Maryland," *The News Journal* (Wilmington, Delaware), February 8, 1995, 44. Newspapers.com.

5 Sam Lacy, "How Can They Select the Greatest," *Baltimore Afro-American*, April 25, 1970, 8. ProQuest Historical Newspapers: Black Newspapers.

6 Peter Dreier and Robert Elias, *Baseball Rebels: The Players, People, and Social Movements That Shook Up the Game and Changed America* (Lincoln: University of Nebraska Press, 2022): 33-34, 37.

7 Larry David Brimmer, *Accused: The Trials of the Scottsboro Boys: Lies, Prejudice, and the Fourteenth Amendment* (New York: Calkins Creek, 2019): 78.

8 Sam Lacy, "The Prince and the Thou A to Z," *Baltimore Afro-American*, May 3, 1975, 9. ProQuest Historical Newspapers: Black Newspapers.

9 Lawrence Sykes, "Decatur Portfolio: Notes on a Passing," *Callaloo* 6 (May 1979): 53.

10 Bryan Marquard, "His Art Mined 'Haunting Experiences'," *Boston Globe*, October 4, 2020, B1.

11 Marquard, "His Art Mined 'Hunting Experiences'," B5.

12 "Lawrence Francis Sykes," https://www.davisofboston.com/obituary/Lawrence-Sykes.

13 "Social Notes," *California Eagle*, December 4, 1947, 10. Newspapers.com.

14 "Pakistan Honors CARE Director," *Evening Sun* (Baltimore), November 7, 1968, 5. Newspapers.com.

15 Biographical information on the Sykes children comes, in part, from the following: "Charles Sykes," email to the author, August 5, 2023.

16 "Alice Sykes, former Baltimore teacher," *Baltimore Sun*, August 11, 1992, 11. Newspapers.com; "Obituary," Saint Francis Xavier Roman Catholic Church, August 1992.

ABOUT THE AUTHOR

Bernard McKenna is an English professor at the University of Delaware and the author of *The Baltimore Black Sox: A Negro Leagues History, 1913-1936*. He founded the Baltimore chapter of the Society for American Baseball Research (SABR) and is a native of Baltimore City.